making Scripture memorable

Over 150 Bible Memory Activities for Families at Home or Church

Susan L. Lingo

STANDARD PUBLISHING

Cincinnati, Ohio

Dedication

I meditate on your precepts
and consider your ways.
I delight in your decrees;
I will not neglect your word.
Psalm 119:15, 16

Making Scripture Memorable
© 2000 Susan L. Lingo

Published by Standard Publishing, Cincinnati, Ohio
A division of Standex International Corporation

Credits

Produced by Susan L. Lingo, Bright Ideas Books™
Cover design by Liz Howe
Illustrated by Sam Thiewes

07 06 05 04 03 02 01 00 5 4 3 2 1
ISBN 0-7847-1110-0
Printed in the United States of America

CONTENTS

EVERYONE LOVES GOOD FRUIT!

God especially loves good fruit—when that good fruit is grown from the seeds of Scripture that we plant in our hearts and minds! Think of how a seed grows: it sends down roots, becomes firmly established, then begins to grow healthy leaves and buds that finally produce a harvest of good fruit used to nourish others and grow more fruit. Sound like God's Word? You bet! When we take time to learn, recall, and put God's Word to work in our lives, we produce all the spiritual fruit that Galatians 5:22, 23 teaches—plus a bushel full of other powerful, life-giving fruit!

Making Scripture Memorable is the first book of its kind because it encourages whole families and churches to stay on the "same page" learning Scripture through lively, age-appropriate, thought-provoking ways. Fun activities, songs, craft ideas, discussions, and word studies are offered for three age groups from preschool and kindergarten to elementary kids to youth and adults. Use the monthly Scripture activities in Sunday school classes, as adult word studies, or as fabulous family devotions. This is Scripture that all ages can learn, remember, and apply in their lives—guaranteed! Don't spend your time trying just to make Scripture "stick" for a moment, make it *memorable* for a lifetime!

HOW TO USE MAKING SCRIPTURE MEMORABLE

Making Scripture Memorable is incredibly simple to use! Each month a new verse or series of verses is introduced and are memorably linked to the months in which they appear either by holidays or seasons. Four monthly activities are presented for every age level every month to make planning a snap! Just choose and use the age levels you desire and teach according to the weeks of the month. Here are the features for every month's worth of Scripture learning fun:

➤ **Monthly Introduction**—Provides valuable background information, Scripture tips, the Secret Scripture Signal, and any reproducible patterns needed for that month.

➤ **Weekly Activities**—Four weeks' worth of short activities for each of three age levels. Week one is *Sowing the Word* (learning the words and any word tricks for recall); week two is *Knowing the Word* (understanding the verse); week three is *Growing the Word* (application of the verse); and week four is *Showing the Word* (prayer and challenge as well as valuable reviews).

➤ **Weekly Word Journal**—A four-week word study to help teens and adults assimilate the meaning of verses, explore more biblical concepts, and write their feelings and thoughts about portions of Scripture.

➤ **Fun Family Activities**—A family handout containing four weeks' worth of review and reinforcement fun. What a bonus!

➤ **Scripture Cards**—Reproducible cards for monthly verses in each age level. Great for games, reviews, and memorization!

So what are you waiting for? Get going and growing the good fruit of God's Word ... and put the harvest to work in your lives!

SCRIPTURE LOG

Photocopy the Scripture Log, then have learners write the verses they're memorizing in the left-hand column. Each time a learner reviews a verse, have her write a check mark in the right-hand column. See if you can fill all the squares!

REVIEW ROCKET

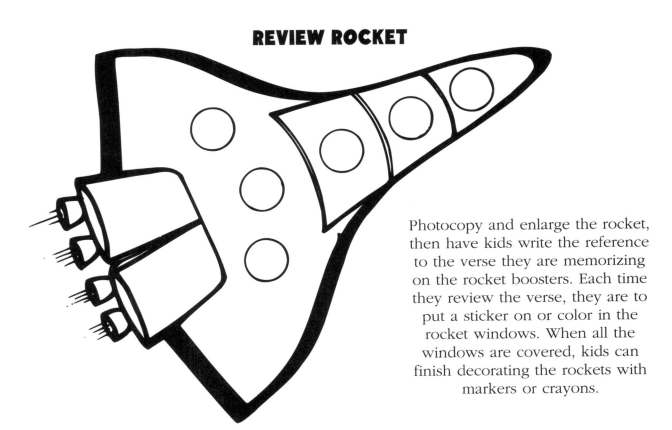

Photocopy and enlarge the rocket, then have kids write the reference to the verse they are memorizing on the rocket boosters. Each time they review the verse, they are to put a sticker on or color in the rocket windows. When all the windows are covered, kids can finish decorating the rockets with markers or crayons.

New Creations   2 Corinthians 5:17-19

PLANTING THE SEEDS

Ring in the New Year! Another year has gone, and a new year has arrived! Just think of the big celebrations that accompany the end of the year and the beginning of a new one. People party, play games, and make resolutions about their behavior and habits. With the advent of a fresh new year, people feel the promise of tomorrow and the hope of change. Although Christians have as much fun as anyone at New Year's, we realize the most joyous change comes from embracing Jesus as Lord of our lives and the promise and hope that come from loving and serving him. Second Corinthians 5:17-19 are wonderful verses that help us celebrate this new time of year and remind us where real change and celebration lie: in the hearts of those who know, love, and follow Jesus!

Pre K–K (2 Corinthians 5:17). Young children especially get caught up in the exuberance of the new year and the excitement that change and newness bring. Though 2 Corinthians 5:17 is a longer verse for children this age to learn, it lends itself well to songs, rhymes, and the concepts of old and new. Look for ways to compare and contrast new and old foods, articles of clothing, toys, and cars. Remember to reinforce that with new life in Jesus comes new ways of thinking and acting, which include being kind to others, sharing, and helping. If very young kids are having trouble learning a verse with so many words, carve the verse down to this precious nugget: *The old has gone, the new has come—Jesus loves us, everyone!*

Elementary (2 Corinthians 5:17). Kids in elementary school experience change with each new school year. And they're familiar with the kinds of change that new rules, new teachers, and new friends bring about! For most kids, a new school year means an opportunity to begin again with a blank slate and to make a fresh start. Consequently, 2 Corinthians 5:17 is a verse kids can identify with— they just need to explore and understand the types of change that come with new lives in Christ; changes such as speaking kind words, being more thoughtful of others, taking some responsibility in learning God's Word, and placing faith in him! The length of this verse should be just right for remembering, and the concepts of old and new can be explored through comparison lists, observation of physical items, and more conceptual changes, such as with attitudes and feelings. Help kids realize that newness from Jesus starts in our hearts and attitudes—and makes us look shiny new on the outside!

Youth/Adult (2 Corinthians 5:17-19). Perhaps there's no group quite as cynical and unsure about change as older youth and adults. After years of seeing promise not measure up to expectations and new beginnings turn rusty from neglect, this age group is especially resistant to change. Use 2 Corinthians 5:17, 18 to reestablish hope and confidence in newness by helping learners recognize that this new change is not from anything we do or instigate, but from God's reconciliation through Christ! The change is natural and wonderful, and it happens when we truly love and obey the Lord. Stress that it's always important to read the Scripture just before and after the verses they're learning to understand the context of the verses and to help them recall their words and meaning.

SECRET SCRIPTURE SIGNAL

Each month a new Scripture signal is suggested as a fun way of signaling someone in your church or family to repeat the month's key verse! For this month's Scripture signal, you'll need a bell to "ring out the old" and "ring in the new." Each time you ring a bell or hear a bell ring, repeat the verse to yourself, or if you're with someone else, repeat the verse with that person.

GARDENING TIPS

- Copy and cut out the Scripture Cards on page 128. Have youth and adults tape the card in their cars to review at stoplights.
- Get everyone involved in a fix-up project around the church or home to demonstrate the old becoming new.
- Look for opposites in this verse and check out the "new-old-new" pattern of the words.

Therefore,	**the old has gone,**
if anyone is in Christ,	**the new has come!**
he is a new creation;	**2 Corinthians 5:1 7**

WEEK 1—SOWING THE WORD

Form a circle and invite children to name things that make them happy, such as sunshine, Mommy or Daddy, or a favorite toy or food. Then explain that God's Word makes us happy, too. Remind children that God's Word is true and helps us live happy lives. Explain that today you'll learn a happy song about our new lives in Jesus and that the words come from 2 Corinthians 5:17 in the Bible.

Sing the following action song to the tune of "Twinkle, Twinkle Little Star." Sing slowly at first so children become familiar with the words and accompanying actions.

> ***Therefore, if we love God's Son,*** (Cover heart with hands.)
> ***We're a new creation.*** (Clap and turn around one time.)
> ***The old has gone, the new has come—***(Point thumbs over shoulders, then in front of you.)
> ***Jesus loves us, everyone!*** (Shout this line.)
> ***Therefore, if we love God's Son,*** (Cover heart with hands.)
> ***We're a new creation.*** (Clap and turn around one time.)

Repeat the verse three times, having kids echo back portions. Remind children that when we love Jesus, we have happy, new lives in him. If you desire, copy the words to the song to send home to practice. Send home the Fun Family Activities from page 15.

WEEK 2—KNOWING THE WORD

Collect an interesting array of old and new items, such as new shoes and worn shoes, new socks and socks with holes, or green leaves and withered leaves. Place the items in the center of the room and seat children around them. Sing the Scripture song from last week two times, then invite kids to sort the items into old and new piles.

When the items are separated, ask children which they'd rather have: an old sock or a new one and why. Discuss which items seem more useful and more valuable and why. Then explain that sometimes old things are fine, such as old shirts for painting in. But old habits or old ways of acting unkindly aren't good. Explain that because Jesus loves us, he wants to give us shiny, new lives that are loving and helpful to others. Remind children that when we love Jesus and follow him, we're new creations—the old has gone and the new has come!

Repeat 2 Corinthians 5:17 two times, then end by singing the Scripture song once more.

Therefore, if anyone is in Christ, he is a new creation; the old has gone, the new has come! 2 Corinthians 5:17

WEEK 3—GROWING THE WORD

Begin by singing the Scripture song for 2 Corinthians 5:17 and repeating the verse two times. Then invite children to sit in a circle and hand each child a sandwich bag half filled with small crackers, cookies, or pieces of fruit. Remind children that when we love Jesus, we're new creations who act in new, loving ways. To put that into practice, kids will have a chance to show their new lives by showing love to each other.

Invite children to mill around the room handing out treats to one another and saying kind words such as "Jesus loves you" or "You're my friend." Tell children they can put some of the treats they're given in their bags to munch later.

After a few minutes, have children sit in a circle, then say a prayer thanking Jesus for your new lives and for the kindness we can show others. Let kids nibble their treats, then end by repeating 2 Corinthians 5:17 two more times and singing the Scripture song as kids skip or hop in a circle.

WEEK 4—SHOWING THE WORD

Repeat 2 Corinthians 5:17 two times. Then tell children that you'll be making cute new creations to remind everyone that we're wonderful new creations in Christ.

Hand each child a cardboard tissue tube and two 12-inch squares of colored tissue or wrapping paper. Tape the squares of paper to the inside ends of the tubes to make "wings" that can be stuffed inside the tube to make a "caterpillar" or pulled out to make "butterflies." Use crayons or markers to decorate the tubes and to add smiling faces.

As you work, explain how fuzzy caterpillars change into beautiful butterflies and trade their old lives for fluttery new ones! Remind children that we're changed into new creations when we love Jesus and, though we don't change the way we look, we do change the ways we feel and act! Encourage children to tell what loving things they could do for others, such as sharing, helping, saying kind words, and giving warm hugs.

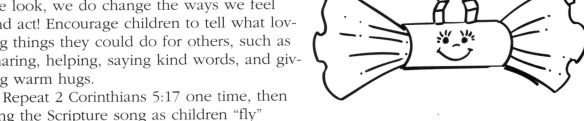

Repeat 2 Corinthians 5:17 one time, then sing the Scripture song as children "fly" around the room with their butterflies and celebrate being new creations in Christ. Then end with this cute rhyme about old and new creations:

Fuzzy little caterpillar, once your life was old— (Tuck wings in tubes.)
Now you are a butterfly, big and bright and bold! (Untuck and flap the wings.)

WEEK 1—SOWING THE WORD

Photocopy the six cards for 2 Corinthians 5:17 from page 7 on stiff paper. Make a set for each child plus one extra.

Place the cards in order on the chalk rail or floor and have kids repeat the verse three times. Tell kids to close their eyes. Remove one of the cards. See if anyone can remember which verse portion is missing, then replace it and repeat the verse. Continue removing one, two, or three portions and have kids identify the missing parts.

When you've replaced the portions of the verse, point out that what you've just done is "lumped" the verse into several parts to make it easier to remember. Challenge kids to close their eyes and visualize each lumped portion. End by having kids get into pairs and see if they can repeat the verse to their partners with only one or two "helps."

Hand each child a set of cards for 2 Corinthians 5:17 to take home and practice playing with family and friends. Keep the Scripture Cards to use during the following weeks and send home the Fun Family Activities from page 15.

WEEK 2—KNOWING THE WORD

Before class, enlarge and photocopy the questionnaire below for each child. Then set up the Scripture Cards from last week.

Have kids repeat the verse two times using the cards, then invite kids to remove one card at a time and continue repeating it. Continue until the verse cards are gone but kids can still repeat the verse.

Form pairs or trios and hand a questionnaire and pen to each child. Be sure each group has a Bible! Challenge kids to look up the references and answer the questions. When the questionnaire is finished, have kids share their answers with the entire class. Discuss what changes we experience in our new lives with Jesus and how those changes help make us stronger, more loving, and more faithful to everyone.

End by having each small group repeat 2 Corinthians 5:17 aloud for the class.

LIVIN' LARGE & NEW IN CHRIST! WHAT DOES IT ALL MEAN?

❧ **When we love Jesus, what do we have?** (Galatians 5:22, 23)

❧ **Why do we need new lives in Christ?** (Romans 3:23)

❧ **What does Jesus give us in our new lives?** (Philippians 4:13)

❧ **How do we work and serve in our new lives?** (Colossians 3:17)

Therefore, if anyone is in Christ, he is a new creation; the old has gone, the new has come! 2 Corinthians 5:17

WEEK 3—GROWING THE WORD

Find a large, branched twig and place it in a pot or can. Use florists' clay, modeling dough, or plaster to hold it in place so it looks like a potted tree. Have construction paper, markers, and tape ready.

Gather kids around the bare tree and repeat 2 Corinthians 5:17 two times. Have kids tell ways an old tree is different from a bushy new tree. Then remind kids that when we're changed into new creations through Jesus' love, we act in new ways. Tell kids that you'll help turn this old tree into a new creation to remind others about our new lives in Jesus. Have kids tear out paper leaves and write encouraging words on the leaves, such as "We're new creations in Christ," "Love and obey Jesus," and "Nothing is impossible with Jesus!" Challenge each person to make three leaves. Then tape the leaves to the tree branches until the tree has become a bushy new creation.

Let your kids present their new creation to another class to read and enjoy. Repeat 2 Corinthians 5:17 for the class, then lead them in a prayer thanking Jesus for helping us become changed through his love.

WEEK 4—SHOWING THE WORD

Make a second set of Scripture Cards for 2 Corinthians 5:17 (see page 7) and place the sets in two scrambled piles in the center of the room. Form two teams and make a relay race out of placing the cards in their correct order so the entire verse can be read. The first team to correctly assemble and repeat the verse is the winner. Repeat the relay a few times with new teams. Then end with high fives and repeat the verse together as a group.

Remind kids that being new creations in Christ means acting, thinking, and feeling differently. Tell kids they'll make huge paper dolls of themselves to remind them of the new changes in their lives. Have kids help each other trace their outlines on rolls of white shelf paper. Cut out the paper dolls and decorate them. Then write new ways of acting, feeling, and speaking on the dolls. For example, on the lips write: "Speak encouraging words." Or write "Step out of your way to help others!" on the feet. Finally, write the first part of 2 Corinthians 5:17 across the "shirts" of the dolls.

When the dolls are complete, read aloud the new ways of thinking, acting, speaking, and feeling. Challenge kids to put their new plans into action, then end with a prayer asking for Jesus' help in guiding their new lives.

WEEK 1—SOWING THE WORD

Write each of the three verses from 2 Corinthians 5:17-19 on a large sheet of newsprint and tape the sheets to the wall or a door. Read the verses aloud two times, then point out how verses 18 and 19 are similar. Explain how, in each of these verses, God reconciles us to him and how we're to take the message of reconciliation into the world. Underline on the newsprint the phrases "to himself," "through/in Christ," and "ministry/message of reconciliation" in both of the verses. (Physically visualizing these similarities will help with verse recall later.) Ask for other similarities and word patterns in the verses, such as the opposites of *old* and *new, gone* and *come.*

Have everyone repeat the verses two more times as they think of these patterns and look at the words on the newsprint. Pass out the Weekly Word Journal from page 14 and encourage learners to underline the patterns in the verses as you've done, then complete the first week of their journal pages at home.

WEEK 2—KNOWING THE WORD

Before class, cut out a variety of colored hearts. Be sure you have twice as many hearts as there are participants. Place the hearts on a table and invite each person to choose a heart. Now tell participants they can trade their hearts for different ones or keep what they have. Repeat the exchange again, then briefly discuss why people chose the hearts they did and, if they exchanged hearts, why. Have a volunteer read aloud 2 Corinthians 5:17, 18. Explain that God chose to give us new life through Jesus just as he chose to reconcile us to himself through Jesus. Point out that having new lives in Christ means making choices. Then read the verses before and after 2 Corinthians 5:17, 18 to get the verses in complete context.

Ask participants what choices they must make in their new lives that they didn't make before or chose wrongly in their old lives before loving Christ. Discuss why choices in our new lives are important and how those choices might reflect our reconciliation to God. Tell participants to keep the paper hearts in their Bibles to remind them how loving Jesus helps us make good choices in our new lives. End by repeating 2 Corinthians 5:17-19 two times.

Therefore, if anyone is in Christ, he is a new creation; the old has gone, the new has come! ... 2 Corinthians 5:17-19

WEEK 3—GROWING THE WORD

Form two groups for a quick game of New Life Role Play. Designate one side the Old Lifers and the other group the New Lifers. Read the situations below and have each group choose one or two members to act out responses depending on whether they have "old lives" or "new lives in Christ."

- ❧ *You overhear gossip about a friend.*
- ❧ *Your supervisor (or teacher) asks you to be untruthful about a project.*
- ❧ *You receive a tax refund you weren't entitled to.*
- ❧ *You see someone on the street needing help.*
- ❧ *A careless teenager just ran into your new sports car.*

With participants still in their groups, have them discuss briefly the responsibilities that come along with our new lives in Christ and our reconciliation to God and how those responsibilities affect our responses to different situations and people. Ask the following questions, then end by repeating 2 Corinthians 5:17-19 two times.
- ❧ **How can we demonstrate to others that we've changed?**
- ❧ **What can we do to thank God for his gift of reconciliation?**

WEEK 4—SHOWING THE WORD

Invite several trios of volunteers to each repeat a portion of 2 Corinthians 5:17-19. Then ask everyone to read Matthew 28:19, 20. Briefly discuss how the Great Commission and 2 Corinthians 5:17-19 are similar. Ask what things we're commanded to do in our walk with the Lord (baptizing others; teaching others to obey; and witnessing about Jesus, our new life in him, and our reconciliation with God). Point out how both of these Scripture passages focus on responsibilities and commands in our new lives in Christ.

Ask participants to turn to a friend and tell one way they can help someone this week learn about the message of reconciliation through Christ and how they can receive Christ's gift of forgiveness, love, and new life.

End with a prayer asking for God's help in allowing us to be powerful witnesses to our new lives in Christ.

January

WEEK 1

Read Colossians 1:22; Romans 3:21-24; 5:1, 10 on reconciliation and justification, then answer the questions below.

❧ What's the difference between being reconciled and being justified?

_____

_____

_____

❧ Why is it good that we don't need to earn reconciliation or justification?

_____

_____

_____

❧ If you could choose only one, would you rather be reconciled or justified? Why?

_____

_____

WEEK 2

Read 2 Corinthians 5:17, 18, then answer the following questions.

❧ What do you think it means to be "in Christ"?

_____

_____

❧ How does being in Christ help us live new lives? help us draw nearer to God?

_____

_____

❧ How do we know when we're in Christ as opposed to merely "beside Christ"?

_____

_____

WEEK 3

Read 2 Corinthians 5:17-19; Galatians 5:22-26; Colossians 1:10-14; Ephesians 4:1-6, 22-32 to discover what new life in Christ brings.

❧ What does new life in Christ entail?

_____

_____

❧ How do we respond to newness in Christ, and what difference does it make in our work, relationships, and faith?

_____

_____

❧ Can we have new life in Christ if we don't see changes in our attitudes, behavior, and words? Explain.

_____

_____

WEEK 4

Read 2 Corinthians 5:17, 18. According to the verses, the old has already gone and the new has *already come*.

❧ How does it feel to see and live one of God's promises right now and not wait for it until some future time?

_____

_____

❧ In what ways does knowing we're living God's promise now affect our level of hope, faith, and assurance in God's Word?

_____

_____

❧ How can you express thanks for God's living promise this week?

_____

_____

January

WEEK 1—Scripture Posters

Make a set of three or four family resolutions that have the words *God, Jesus,* or *the Bible* in them. Have family members write each resolution on a sheet of poster board, then use crayons, markers, paints, bingo daubers, foil, glitter, sequins, and other eye-catching materials to decorate the posters. Add 2 Corinthians 5:17 to each poster. Hang the posters around the house to read often, changing their positions every week. Take time often to assess how the family is doing in keeping the new resolutions.

WEEK 2—Cheese, Please!

Whip up a new creation in the kitchen with this yummy recipe for family fondue! Over a double boiler, melt 2 cups of cheddar cheese, 1 cup of mozzarella cheese, and ½ cup of pizza sauce. Be sure everyone has a chance to measure, grate, or stir the cheese! When the cheeses are melted, have family members take turns dipping bread, crackers, rolls, or pretzels in the pot and munching the treats as you chat about how God's Word feeds and helps nourish us in our new lives in Christ. See if each person can repeat 2 Corinthians 5:17 before they take a dip in the cheesy sauce!

WEEK 3—Notice the New!

Pick a day for a car ride through the city and country. Rainy days are especially fun for this activity! Hand each person a paper and marker. As you drive along, write "old" things you see on one half of the papers and "new" things you see on the other half. You might include old cars, buildings, dead trees, and litter on the old list and new houses, bikes, and flowers on the new portion. Young children may draw pictures of what they see. When you have at least six things listed or drawn on each side, stop for fresh French fries and compare your lists. Remind everyone that our old lives before loving Jesus were sad and filled with sin but our new lives are happy and filled with being kind to others, helping, sharing, and learning God's Word.

WEEK 4—Just Like New

Have everyone in the family decorate an old glove to wear for cleaning. Make sure the gloves are cotton or a polyester blend. Cotton gardening gloves work great for this spiffy craft! Decorate the gloves with permanent markers and use tacky craft glue to attach plastic jewels for rings, fake fingernails, or other fun touches. When the gloves are dry and ready to use, have a family clean-up party as you turn things new and shiny! Use the gloves to polish furniture and shine windows or to straighten things out of place. When you're done cleaning, serve crackers and juice and discuss how much better everything feels when it's like new, including our lives! End by having everyone repeat 2 Corinthians 5:17 and giving each other high fives.

Fun Family Activities

GOD'S LOVE

Romans 8:37-39

PLANTING THE SEEDS

What do we never seem to have enough of yet joyously give away? Love! Love is what makes the world sing in tunes not always understood but universally felt. Love is the recipe for compassion, kindness, and forgiveness; the remedy for unhappiness, anger, and hate. Yet often we feel there's not enough love coming our way. Who will love us when we're our most unlovable? God! Romans 8:38, 39 assure us that nothing can separate us from the love of God that is ours in Christ. As Valentine's Day approaches and we're filled with thoughts of love abundant or love lacking, Romans 8:37-39 is the perfect Scripture to learn and put into action in our lives!

PRE K–K (Romans 8:39). Young children adore Valentine's Day and all its colorful hearts, hugs, and happy smiles. Make the most of this warm time of year by teaching young children the short portion of Romans 8:39 that teaches about God's powerful love and how it never leaves us—even when we forget to brush our teeth or spill our milk!

ELEMENTARY (Romans 8:38, 39). Elementary-aged kids often shy away from the subject of love—even at Valentine's Day! After all, Aunt Martha's kisses can make anyone squirm! But it's important for kids in first through fifth grade to realize that God's love is unconditional, complete, and unending—and instead of embarrassment, it provides security and power! Romans 8:38, 39 provides plenty of great imagery that will make this Scripture easy and fun to learn.

YOUTH/ADULT (Romans 8:37-39). Older learners know that God loves them; after all, they've heard the same theme for years! But encouraging them to really *feel* and *understand* the power and peace of God's eternal love is the most wonderful gift you can offer during this season of love. Romans 8:37-39 may be a bit long, but the three verses flow together smoothly and logically, and the boost of knowing that we're more than conquerors will help older learners begin to recognize the power in God's perfect love.

February

SECRET SCRIPTURE SIGNAL

Each month a new Scripture signal is suggested as a fun way of signaling some-one in your church or family to repeat the month's key verse! For this month's Scripture signal, cover your heart as a gesture of love. Each time you or someone else covers his heart, repeat Romans 8:39 or verses 37, 38, and 39.

GARDENING TIPS

❥ Let kids and adults illustrate their verses with symbols that will help them recall the words.

❥ Cut out the Scripture Cards (pages 126-128) for each age level and make take-home puzzles.

❥ Tape the Scripture Cards to placemats and have family members each repeat the verse during every meal for a week.

WEEK 1—SOWING THE WORD

Before starting this activity, enlarge and photocopy the pictures for Romans 8:39 on page 17. Cut them out, color them, and tape them to a sheet of poster board, then add the words to the verse to the poster. (See illustration.) Tape the Scripture rebus poster to the wall or door.

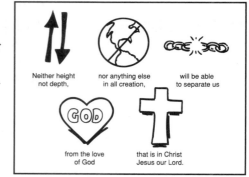

Have children stand beside the poster and repeat Romans 8:39 as you point to the pictures. For example, point to the up arrow for the word *height*. Repeat the verse two times pointing to the pictures, then encourage children to repeat the verse with you as you point.

Explain that this verse tells us that God's love will never leave us and can't be taken away. Then act out the verse as follows.

Neither height nor depth, (Stand on tiptoe, then bend low.)
Nor anything else in all creation, (Hold your arms in big circle.)
Will be able to separate us (Lock your fingers, then pull them apart.)
From the love of God (Put your hands over your hearts.)
That is in Christ Jesus our Lord. (Make a cross with your fingers.)

Repeat the actions and verse two times, then tell children that nothing can take away God's love for them and that nothing can take away your love for them. End by giving everyone a hug. Save the Scripture rebus poster to use during the next few weeks. Send home the Fun Family Activities from page 25.

WEEK 2—KNOWING THE WORD

Before this activity, collect a button for each child. You'll also need thin elastic cord, safety pins, a marker, red construction paper, and tacky craft glue. Cut the elastic cord into 8-inch lengths.

Have children gather by the rebus poster and repeat the verse several times as you (or they) point to the pictures. Then act out the Scripture verse using the motions learned last week. Remind children that nothing in the world can take away God's love that is ours through Jesus.

Tell children you'll make fun hearts of love to show that God's love stays with us no matter what! Help kids thread the thin elastic cord through the button holes, then tie the ends in a secure knot. Glue a 1-inch paper heart to the button, then slide a safety pin through the knot. Pin the spring-back hearts to children's shirts. When the heart-buttons are gently tugged, they'll spring back. Let

Neither height nor depth, nor anything else in all creation, will be able to separate us from the love of God.... Romans 8:39

children "sproing" their button-hearts several times as you explain that God's love stays with them just as the hearts do!

End by saying a prayer of thanks for God's unending love. Then repeat Romans 8:39 two more times and let children spring their hearts when you repeat the portion about never being separated from God's love.

WEEK 3—GROWING THE WORD

Collect an aluminum-foil pie tin for each child. You'll also need pink and red construction-paper hearts, tape, and a copy of the Scripture Card for Romans 8:39 from page 126.

Begin by repeating Romans 8:39 using the rebus poster, then act out the verse two times. Remind children that nothing can take away the love of the Lord! Then lead children in repeating and clapping the phrase: "Nothing can take away the love of the Lord!" Continue clapping and repeating the line for several repetitions.

Hand out paper hearts and the foil pie tins. Have children turn the tins upside-down, then tape the paper hearts to the bottoms of the tins. After several hearts are in place, tape the Scripture Card for Romans 8:39 on top of the hearts. Invite children to tap and bang on their tins as you repeat: "Nothing can take away the love of the Lord!"

End by telling children that God loves us when we're good, when we make mistakes, and when we're happy or sad and that it's important to remember that God's love will never leave us. Repeat the actions and verse two times, then challenge children to give their pretty tins to someone they love as a reminder of God's unending love for all people.

WEEK 4—SHOWING THE WORD

Cut out three to five paper hearts for each child and hide the hearts around the room. Gather children in front of the rebus poster and invite them to take turns pointing to the pictures as you repeat the words to Romans 8:39. Continue until every child has had a turn to point to the pictures.

Ask children what will never be taken from us. Then invite children to go on a heart hunt. When the paper hearts have been found, tell children that just as we found hearts around the room, we find God's love in all our lives! Remind kids that God's love is forever, then invite them to tell how God's love makes them feel. Share a prayer thanking God for his never-ending love, then say a corporate "amen" and blow God a kiss upward. End by repeating Romans 8:39 two times. Let children each take home several paper hearts to give to friends and family to remind them that we can find God's ever-present love every day of our lives.

WEEK 1—SOWING THE WORD

Before this activity, enlarge and photocopy the rebus pictures from page 17. Color and cut out the pictures and tape them to a sheet of poster board, then add the words to the verse as shown in the illustration. Hang the poster.

Gather kids by the poster and point to the pictures as you read Romans 8:38, 39. For example, when you say "For I am convinced that neither death nor life," point to the tombstone and the flower. Repeat the verse two times.

Tell kids that this verse tells us something very important about God's love, then ask what kids think that is. Guide kids to understand that Romans 8:38, 39 tells us that nothing can take away God's love that is ours through Jesus! Then ask kids to identify pairs of opposites in the two verses such as *death* and *life* or *height* and *depth*. Circle the pairs on the poster in different colors. If there's time, challenge kids to make up other opposites such as "Neither storms nor sunshine can separate us from God's love."

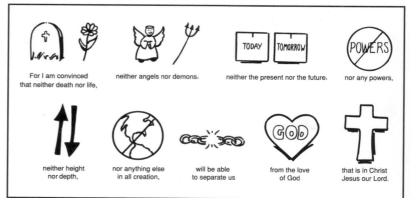

End by inviting pairs of kids to lead in repeating the verse and pointing to the pictures on the poster. Continue until everyone has had a turn to lead or point. Then close with a prayer thanking God for his unending love through Jesus.

Keep the poster to use for the next several weeks and send home the Fun Family Activities from page 25.

WEEK 2—KNOWING THE WORD

Gather kids by the Scripture rebus poster and invite volunteers to point to the pictures as you repeat the verse three times. Then have kids form small groups of three or four and hand each group a sheet of paper.

Have kids list times they might have been afraid they'd lose love, such as when they told a lie or got mad over a lost toy. Have them write down or draw as many situations as they can in five minutes, then call time and have them share their lists. Each time someone names a situation that hasn't been named before, have kids leap to their feet and shout, "Nothing can take away the love of the Lord!"

Remind kids that God's love will never stop or be taken away because Jesus loves us and has forgiven us even during times when we're most unlovable! Ask kids:

➤ **How does God's unending love affect how you feel and treat others?**

... Neither height nor depth, nor anything else in all creation, will be able to separate us from the love of God.... Romans 8:38, 39

❧ **In what ways does God's perfect love give us hope? security? peace?**

End by repeating Romans 8:38, 39 two times, then end with a lively cheer to express your thanks to God for his perfect love!

WEEK 3—GROWING THE WORD

Photocopy the Scripture Card for Romans 8:38, 39 from page 127 for each child. You'll also need construction paper, markers, scissors, glue, ribbon, and lace.

Gather kids by the rebus poster and repeat the verse once using the pictures. Turn the poster over and invite pairs of kids to repeat Romans 8:38, 39. If they need help, have kids ask friends. Continue until everyone has had a turn repeating the verse. When you're done, have pairs give each other high fives.

Remind kids that God's love is always with us and that means we have plenty of love to share with others—not just on Valentine's Day but *every* day! Ask kids who they can show love to this week and how they can tell someone else about God's unending love.

Have each person make a special valentine to share with someone. Use construction paper and the other craft items to decorate heart-shaped cards, then glue the Scripture Card for Romans 8:38, 39 to the valentine. Challenge kids to hand their gifts of love to someone special, then end by repeating Romans 8:38, 39 two times.

WEEK 4—SHOWING THE WORD

Before this activity, purchase clear vinyl from a craft store. This vinyl can be colored with markers, then stuck in a window as a static stick-on. You'll need an 8-inch square for each child. You'll also need a Scripture Card for every two kids. Cut the cards into six pieces and place each group of pieces in an envelope.

Have kids form pairs and hand each pair an envelope. Repeat Romans 8:38, 39 two times, then challenge kids to put their verses together as quickly as they can. When the verses are complete, have partners repeat them aloud.

Ask kids how they can put God's Word to work this week, such as by telling others about God's love or about Jesus' forgiveness. Then let kids write Romans 8:38, 39 on the vinyl pieces. Place white paper under the vinyl, then use markers to write the words and add decorations around the edges. Challenge kids to place the verses on their bathroom mirrors and read them each morning and night for the next two weeks to remind them that just as the vinyl sticks to the mirrors, God's love sticks to each of us!

Youth/Adult February

WEEK 1—SOWING THE WORD

Photocopy the Scripture Card from Romans 8:37-39 from page 128 for each learner. Be sure to provide pens.

Distribute the Scripture Cards and read aloud the verses two times. Then point out that these verses have a pattern of *neither-nor* and opposites. Note that three *neither-nors* are followed by a *nor*, then a single *neither-nor* is followed by the last *nor*. Circle the pairs of opposites and underline the word *neither* once each time it appears and the word *nor* twice wherever it appears. Then point out that these three verses tell us three things we are: verse 37 tells us we're "more than conquerors," verse 38 says we're "convinced," and verse 39 says we're loved.

Have learners repeat the verses two more times looking at the patterns and imagining the opposites and the three things we are. Then have each person turn to someone nearby, tell the three things we are, and repeat the verses.

Hand out the Weekly Word Journal from page 24 to be completed at home during the coming week.

WEEK 2—KNOWING THE WORD

Before class, cut out small paper hearts and push four inside an uninflated balloon. Blow up and tie off the balloon. Prepare one balloon for every four participants. Be sure you have permanent markers or pens available. Write the words to Romans 8:37-39 on a sheet of newsprint and tape it to the wall or door.

Repeat Romans 8:37-39 two times using the words on the newsprint to help. Then ask what three things these verses tell us we are (as a review of last week's activity). Remind everyone that the verses tell us that we're more than conquerors, convinced, and loved.

Have learners form groups of four and hand each group a marker and a balloon with four hearts inside. Have groups jot their answers to these questions on the balloons:

❧ **Can we turn from God and take away or ignore our love for him? Explain.**
❧ **What situations or things might pull us away from God or cause us to forget or ignore his love for us?**

After a few minutes, have groups share the answers on their balloons, then remind them that Romans 8:37-39 tells us that nothing can truly separate us from God's love through Jesus. We may turn from God, but God never turns from us! Have groups pop their balloons and free the paper hearts inside. Explain that just as the balloon seemed to separate the hearts from us, they couldn't stay that way! God's love can pop through any problem, trouble, or situation, and it stays with us forever!

End by repeating Romans 8:37-39. Have everyone take home a paper heart as a Bible bookmark and a reminder of God's unending love.

... Neither height nor depth, nor anything else in all creation, will be able to separate us from the love of God.... Romans 8:37-39

WEEK 3—GROWING THE WORD

Before this activity, set out construction paper, paper doilies, ribbon, glue, and markers.

Have participants form trios and challenge the groups to repeat Romans 8:37-39, with each group member repeating one of the verses. Switch and repeat the verse again until everyone has repeated each verse.

Then ask small groups to discuss the following questions:

❦ **How can this portion of Scripture encourage our faith? our obedience?**

❦ **In what ways can we demonstrate to others that we're more than conquerors?**

❦ **Why does God want us to remember this passage?**

Explain that since it's Valentine's month, everyone can create an old-fashioned valentine to present to someone as a way of spreading the unending love that God gives us through his grace and through Jesus. Have learners write one sentence about God's love on the card. Remind everyone to give the card to a family member or friend and repeat Romans 8:37-39 for them.

WEEK 4—SHOWING THE WORD

Hand each learner a sheet of paper and a pencil or pen. Repeat Romans 8:37-39 one time in unison, then have volunteers pop up to each say one of the verses. Continue repeating the verses until everyone who wants a chance to do the "popcorn" Scripture has had a turn.

Remind everyone that this portion of Scripture is important because it tells us where we stand in God's love. In addition, how we react to this verse can affect our levels of hope, faith, love for others, and trust in God. Challenge participants to write prayer or praise responses for each verse of Romans 8:37-39. For example, in response to verse 37, someone might write a praise saying, "Because you are all-powerful, Lord, we are more than conquerors!" Someone else might write a prayer request such as, "Dear Lord, please help me remember that I am more than a conqueror through your love."

When the responses are complete, read each verse aloud and have volunteers read their responses for each verse. Challenge everyone to read the verses and the responses twice a day for the following week. Then end with a prayer thanking God for his abundant love.

February

WEEK 1

Read Romans 8:37-39 and think about the saying, "Love conquers all." Then answer these questions.

❧ How does Romans 8:37-39 make this saying true?

_____

_____

❧ In what ways is love our best weapon against self-doubt, hate, and depression?

_____

_____

❧ How can you use God's love *today* to conquer a fear, problem, or doubt?

_____

_____

WEEK 2

Look up the word *separation* in the dictionary, then think of all the things that can be separated and those that can't.

❧ What things might separate you from God though his love is never separated from us?

_____

_____

❧ Name three things you can do to draw nearer to God:

_____

_____

❧ Circle one of the above ways and commit to following it for the next two weeks.

WEEK 3

Romans 8:39 tells us that we're loved through Jesus. Look up the references to find out what else we receive "through Jesus."

❧ 2 Timothy 3:15

_____

❧ Romans 5:17

_____

❧ 1 Thessalonians 5:9

_____

❧ 1 Corinthians 15:57

_____

❧ What's one thing you can give back to Jesus this week to thank him for all we receive through his love?

_____

_____

WEEK 4

Think of the opposites listed in Romans 8:38, 39. The technique of listing opposites to express "everything" in poetic terms is called *merism*. Use merism to write a psalm thanking or praising God for *everything* his love conquers or calms in your life. For example, you might write, "Lord, your love is perfect! It conquers life and death, joy and sadness...." Use the back of this paper if you need more room to write. Then use this psalm as your morning and evening prayer tomorrow as you express your own unending love for God!

_____

_____

_____

_____

_____

_____

_____

_____

February

WEEK 1—Collage Card

Make a family collage card filled with love to mail or present to relatives or close friends of the family. Cut out a large red or pink poster-board heart. On the heart write, "Can you feel the love we're sending? Our love for you is never ending!" Then have each family member draw a picture or write a greeting that expresses happy, warm sentiments. Glue the contributions to the giant card and add Romans 8:38, 39 at the bottom of the card next to your signatures. If you have extra photos, be sure to add a few to your creation!

WEEK 3—Mile Meal

Make this cool snack of "never-ending pizza" by cutting a loaf of French bread in half lengthwise. Place the halves on a cookie sheet and spread pizza sauce and cheese on top. Then have everyone pitch in to write "Romans 8:39" on top of the pizza using pepperoni slices, olives, mushrooms, and peppers. Bake your treat for 20 minutes at 350 degrees or until the cheese is hot and bubbly. As you enjoy your family feast, go around the table and help each other repeat Romans 8:37-39 according to what you've worked on this week. End by sharing a prayer thanking God for his unending love and for the unending love your family celebrates!

WEEK 2—Love Safari

Cut out at least six paper hearts, using different colors of construction paper. Or you may wish to use valentine cards for this hunting game. Write Romans 8:39 on the hearts or cards, then cut them into three pieces each. Hide the pieces in the room or around the house. Invite everyone to go on a "love safari" to find the pieces and assemble them correctly to make the verse. When each puzzle is put together, repeat the verse. Then let family members tape the pieces in place and each keep a heart or card as a reminder that we never have to search and hunt for God's love—it's perfect, complete, and with us forever!

WEEK 4—Where's the End?

Pack a simple lunch and share a hike in the woods or a family stroll in the park as you look for "ends" of things, such as the ends of telephone poles, slides, paths, sidewalks, and trees. (You may have to use your imagination to "see" underground!) When you come to the end of your walk, share your picnic and chat about the fact that all things have beginnings and endings, but that God's love has no end! See if you can name other eternal aspects about God, such as his wisdom, forgiveness, mercy, grace, and power. Then take turns repeating Romans 8:39 (or the portions you learned) as you walk back to the car or house.

Fun Family Activities

HOPE

PLANTING THE SEEDS

Ahhh, can it be March and the long winter quickly sliding past? The merry month of March springs forth sprouting shoots, surprises in the weather, and plenty of springtime hope! After months of dormancy, dullness, and darkened days, March lifts her head to shine the first hints of warm weather, breezes, and the promise of growth. What a perfect month to learn Romans 5:3-5, which speaks of God's love being poured into our hearts just as warm sunshine floods our senses!

PRE K–K (Romans 5:5b). Young children revel in the joy and hope March brings. Why, they can finally play outside without all the trappings of boots and mufflers and can taste the freedom of fresh breezes and a world coming alive after a long stillness. Romans 5:5b is a wonderful portion of Scripture to help young children understand that God pours love and hope into our hearts just as gentle rains fill springtime ponds and puddles!

ELEMENTARY (Romans 5:3-5). Older kids love noticing the nuances and changes March brings and delight in the first hint of new plants peeking through melting snow and slush. They realize the importance of rain producing shoots that produce plants that in turn feed us. Romans 5:3-5 is a great Scripture that speaks of the way hope grows in our hearts and lives. Use these verses to remind kids that hope springs from God's love through the Holy Spirit.

YOUTH/ADULT (Romans 5:3-5). Youth and adults are happy to doff the staleness of winter along with scraping car windows and sidewalks, wading through slush, and persevering through hours of early darkness. March is here, and so are the hopes of springtime freedom and summertime fun! Romans 5:3-5 is a wonderful analogy of the "suffering" of winter giving way to the hope of spring in the same way that God's love gives way to hope in our spirits.

SECRET SCRIPTURE SIGNAL

Each month a new Scripture signal is suggested as a fun way of signaling some-one in your church or family to repeat the month's key verse! The signal for this month is a thumbs-up sign. Each time you give or see a thumbs-up sign, repeat your portion of Romans 5:3-5. Happy spring!

GARDENING TIPS

➤ Use the Scripture wheel from page 47 for elementary kids. Write the words to the verses around the edge of the wheel in small letters, then cover up portions of the verses and see if kids can repeat them.

➤ Have learners of any age list the "sufferings" they may have in winter and the hopes they discover in spring.

➤ Be sure to explain the meanings of *perseverance* and *character* to elemen-tary-aged kids.

WEEK 1—SOWING THE WORD

Spread a plastic shower curtain or tablecloth on the floor and set out several wash tubs half filled with water. Place paper cups beside the tubs. Be sure there's a cup for each child.

Invite children to scoop up and pour out water into the tub. Explain that God pours his love and hope into our hearts just as the water is poured into the tub. As you repeat Romans 5:5b, have children slowly pour cups of water back into the tub. Point out that because God has so much love to give, he pours his love into our hearts through the Holy Spirit. Explain that the Holy Spirit is a special friend that Jesus sent to love and help us, and that God sends love and hope through the Holy Spirit. And when we feel loved, we can hope for happy things and know God will bring them our way!

Have children repeat the verse three times echo-style (in which you repeat a phrase and kids repeat it after you) and once in unison. Write children's names on the cups and save them to use with the wash tubs again next week. Hand out the Fun Family Activities from page 35.

WEEK 2—KNOWING THE WORD

Spread the plastic shower curtain or tablecloth on the floor and set up the paper cups and wash tubs with water again. Make copies of the appropriate Scripture Card from page 126.

Have kids find places at the wash tubs, but before they dip water in their cups, repeat Romans 5:5b two times. Then repeat the verse, adding the actions below.

God (Point upward.)
Has poured out his love (Wiggle fingers like rain falling down.)
Into our hearts (Point to your heart.)
By the Holy Spirit. (Hug yourself.)

Remind children that God has so much love that he pours it into our hearts through the Holy Spirit. As children pour cups of water into the tubs, explain that the Holy Spirit is the friend Jesus sent to love and help us and that God sends his love through the Holy Spirit. Tell children that because we receive so much love and hope from God through the Holy Spirit, we can pass that love on to others. Repeat the verse again. Then have children hold their empty cups over the tub as you pour a cup of water into the first child's cup. Have that child then pour the water into the next cup and so on until the water comes back to you.

Finish by letting children decorate their cups using crayons and markers. Tape the Scripture Cards to the cups. Tell children you'll finish making their cups beautiful next week! End by repeating the action verse two times.

WEEK 3—GROWING THE WORD

You'll need tape and colored construction paper. Cut red, orange, yellow, green, blue, and purple construction paper into 4-by-1-inch strips. Cut a set of rainbow strips for each child.

Have children repeat Romans 5:5b with the accompanying motions they learned last week. Repeat the action verse two times. Then remind children that God sends love and hope through our special friend, the Holy Spirit. Tell children that when we have hope, we can look forward to happy things such as someone to care for us, good food to eat, and warm places to live. Then explain that God sent us the rainbow as a symbol of love and hope that everything will turn out fine!

Hand each child a set of rainbow strips and have kids identify the colors. Then help children tape the strips to the rims of their paper cups from last week, leaving space for their mouths to drink from. As you work, tell children that when they use their cups, they can remember that we have hope because we know God will always love us.

WEEK 4—SHOWING THE WORD

Before this activity, enlarge and photocopy the raindrops from page 27 on light blue paper. You'll need a set of raindrops for each child. Cut the raindrops out and number the raindrops in each set from one to five, then place the sets in envelopes.

Have children repeat Romans 5:5b with the accompanying motions learned earlier. Repeat the verse twice and remind children that because God loves us, we can have happy hopes!

Hand each child a set of raindrops and have them put the drops in the correct order according to the numbers on the drops. Then have kids hold the raindrops in their hands. Repeat the verse, and when you say "has poured out his love," have children "pour" the raindrops from their hands or toss them in the air. Then reassemble the verses by number. Play several times, then end with a prayer thanking God for his wonderful love and the happy hope we find in God's love.

WEEK 1—SOWING THE WORD

Before this activity make a secret-pocket sack by cutting the side from a lunch sack and taping it inside and along the side of a second sack so it looks as if it's part of the sack. Don't tape the top opening—this is the secret opening! Cut out several hearts and place them in the main part of the sack. Then cut out four ovals and write one of these words on each: *suffering, perseverance, character, hope*. Tape the ovals to a string in the order they're listed above. Also, make a photocopy the of Scripture Card for elementary kids from page 127 and the Fun Family Activities from page 35 for each child.

Gather kids and place the sack containing the hearts by you. (Don't let anyone see inside!) Hold up the ovals on the string and repeat Romans 5:3-5, pointing to each oval during the verse. Tell kids this portion of Scripture is all about hope and how it comes from God's love through the Holy Spirit. Have kids repeat the verses with you as they read the ovals.

As you slyly place the string of ovals in the secret pocket, explain that suffering brings about perseverance, character, and hope. Then hold the secret opening closed as you pour out the hearts and repeat Romans 5:5. Explain that we can have a confident hope no matter what happens because God has already poured out his love into our hearts and he will turn even "bad" things into something good. Repeat Romans 5:3-5 two times aloud.

Challenge kids to remember the order of the ovals during the week as you hand each child a Scripture Card to learn and a Fun Family Activities to take home.

WEEK 2—KNOWING THE WORD

Cut out four large, green lily pads (or use paper plates). Write one each of the following words on each lily pad: *suffering, perseverance, character, hope*. Tape the lily pads across the floor and about a foot apart.

Have kids repeat Romans 5:3-5 echo-style with you. Then invite volunteers to repeat the verse by themselves or in pairs. Remind kids that because God loves us, we can have hope—even in times of suffering. Ask:
- **How can suffering lead to positive things such as perseverance, character, and hope?**
- **In what ways does God's love bring hope through the Holy Spirit?**
- **What do you think is meant by "Hope does not disappoint us"?**

Have kids line up at one end of the lily pads. Let kids repeat the verses, and when they come to the words *suffering, perseverance, character,* and *hope,* have them leap from lily pad to lily pad, then complete the verse on the other side. Continue until everyone has hopped; give hints as needed. End with a prayer thanking God for turning things such as suffering and hard times into hopeful situations through his love.

WEEK 3—GROWING THE WORD

You'll need paper plates, tinsel or aluminum foil, tape, scissors, construction paper, cotton balls, and copies of the Scripture Card for Romans 5:3-5 from page 127.

Repeat Romans 5:3-5 echo-style with kids, then have trios each repeat one of the verses. Remind kids that we have hope for the future because God loves us through the Holy Spirit. Ask:

❧ **How can love give us hope?**
❧ **In what ways can we pass love and hope onto others?**
❧ **How does the Holy Spirit help us accomplish this?**

Tell kids that long ago, God placed a rainbow in the sky as his promise never to flood the world again. And that promise gives us hope in God, in his love, and in his Word. Explain that you'll make cool rainbows to give to someone who needs to learn about hope and about God's love. Form pairs and have partners cut a paper plate in half and share the halves. Tape tinsel or thin strips of aluminum foil to the flat sides of the plate halves as "rain." Then tape stretched-out cotton balls above the rain as clouds. Finally, cut construction paper arcs and tape them above the clouds for the rainbows. Write "God gives us happy hopes!" across the rainbows. Then tape the Scripture Cards to the backs of the plates.

WEEK 4—SHOWING THE WORD

Make a pitcher of lemonade drink mix but leave out the sugar. Have sugar ready to add later. You'll need paper cups and straws for this activity.

Set out the pitcher of sour lemonade, the cups, and drinking straws. Invite kids to repeat Romans 5:3-5, then pour a bit of lemonade into their cups. Tell them not to sip until everyone has a cup. Remind kids that God pours love into our hearts just as they poured lemonade into their cups. Then have kids take a sip and wait for their surprised reactions. Explain that sufferings are like sour lemonade—hard to swallow! But God's love sent through the Holy Spirit is sweet and gives us hope, like the hope of sugar being added to the lemonade. Let kids each stir into their lemonade several spoonfuls of sugar. Then ask:

❧ **How does the sugar give you hope of sweeter lemonade? How does God's love give us hope of sweeter things?**
❧ **How does it help to know we can have hope during times of trouble and suffering?**

Share a prayer thanking God for his sweet love, which gives us hope, then have kids finish their lemonade. End by repeating Romans 5:3-5 together.

WEEK I—SOWING THE WORD

Photocopy the Scripture Card for Romans 5:3-5 on page 128 and the Weekly Word Journal from page 34 for each participant. Have pencils available. Also, write Romans 5:3-5 on a sheet of newsprint or poster board and tape it to the wall.

Hand out the Scripture Cards and pencils, then have everyone read Romans 5:3-5. Explain that this long section can be made easier to learn by using "lumping" (putting a verse into portions) and "linking" (tying similar components together). Lump the verse by underlining the following verse portions on the newsprint, then draw arrows to the linked components as in the diagram below.

Not only so, but we also rejoice in our sufferings, because we know that suffering produces perseverance; perseverance, character; and character, hope. And hope does not disappoint us, because God has poured out his love into our hearts by the Holy Spirit, whom he has given us.

Repeat the verse, noting the lumps and links. Explain that these strategies work well when learning longer verses or verses with lists or similar components. Challenge learners to repeat and look at Romans 5:3-5 each day for the next week. Hand out the Weekly Word Journal.

WEEK 2—KNOWING THE WORD

Before this activity, make a copy of the How & What questionnaire below for every four participants. Repeat Romans 5:3-5 two times in unison. Then have everyone turn to a friend and repeat the verses. Form groups of four and distribute the How & What questionnaires. Have groups answer the questions, then invite learners to share their answers. End by offering a prayer for God's help in remembering to trust his provision, guidance, and love enough to have hope in all situations.

HOW & WHAT?

➨ HOW can we rejoice in suffering? WHAT effect does rejoicing even in hard times have on our attitudes? our faith? our hope?

➨ HOW are suffering, perseverance, character, and hope produced through one another? WHAT other values are produced through God's love? the Holy Spirit?

➨ HOW is God's love poured out upon us? WHAT can we do with God's fruitful outpouring of love and hope through the Spirit?

... God has poured out his love into our hearts by the Holy Spirit, whom he has given us. Romans 5:3-5

WEEK 3—GROWING THE WORD

Have learners repeat Romans 5:3-5 one time aloud, then ask for three volunteers to pop up and each repeat one of the verses in this passage. Continue until everyone who wants a turn has had one.

Invite learners to get into three groups and designate one group the perseverance group, one the character group, and the other the hope group. Read the following situations in which suffering may or may not be apparent. Then have each group decide how their trait is produced through the one before.

❥ *You've lost your job and your family is depending on you.*
❥ *You feel sad for no "real" reason—you have the blues.*
❥ *You're struggling in school or work with "making the grade."*
❥ *You don't have any free time because of too many responsibilities.*
❥ *A family member has been diagnosed with a serious illness.*

After you've described possible ways perseverance, character, and hope are achieved through stressful situations, ask learners how God uses his love to promote hope in our hearts and faith in our spirits.

End with a prayer asking for God's help in strengthening your character through faith, trust, hope, and love. Then repeat Romans 5:3-5 two times aloud.

WEEK 4—SHOWING THE WORD

Write the letters S, P, C, and H on a piece of poster board and tape it to the wall or a door. Challenge participants to repeat Romans 5:3-5 to three other people in the room. Then have participants gather by the poster board so they can see the letters. Explain that these letters stand for important words in the verses: Suffering, Perseverance, Character, and Hope.

Have participants brainstorm words for the acronym SPCH that describe how we can respond to God's love and help even in times of stress and suffering. Words might include "Smile, Pray, Cheer, and Happiness." Write the words in lists under each letter.

When you have several words under each letter, go around the room and read each word aloud. Then join hands and explain that it's wonderful to pray Scripture just by using the words God has given us.

Pray Romans 5:3-5 by saying: **Dear Lord, we know you want us to rejoice in our sufferings because we know that suffering produces perseverance; perseverance, character; and character, hope. We thank you that we can trust the hope we have in you and for pouring your love into our hearts by the Holy Spirit, your special gift to us. Amen.**

March

WEEK 1

It's often difficult to understand how suffering can have positive effects. Answer these questions and read them in tough times as a reminder that suffering produces the positive traits we learn about in Romans 5:3, 4.

❧ How can suffering make us stronger? How did Christ suffer? What was the result?

_____

_____

❧ Can we understand true joy without a certain degree of suffering? Explain.

_____

_____

❧ What's one thing you can remember when you're feeling stressed or despondent?

_____

_____

WEEK 2

It's been said that there's no great loss without some small gain, and Romans 5:3-5 tells us that hope is born of hard times and God's love. Now think of several Bible persons who experienced suffering and loss, such as Job (Job 1:1–2:10) or Ruth (Ruth 1:1–4:22).

❧ How did each person cope with loss?

_____

_____

❧ What character traits did each grow?

_____

_____

❧ How did God's love and this person's own faith play a part?

_____

_____

WEEK 3

Romans 5:5 tells us that the Holy Spirit is God's ambassador of love through which we find hope that is never disappointing. Read these verses to explore more about the Holy Spirit's empowering help!

❧ 1 Thessalonians 1:5
❧ John 14:16, 17
❧ Romans 15:13
❧ Colossians 1:8
❧ Galatians 5:22, 23

❧ How can you embrace the Holy Spirit more in your life and put your hope in him?

_____

_____

WEEK 4

Romans 5:3-5 teaches us that we can actually *rejoice* even in the hardest of times, while 1 Thessalonians 5:18 tells us that in *all things* we're to give thanks. Using excerpts from the following Scripture passages, compose a prayer of praise and thanksgiving to God for giving us hope, help, and love in all situations. Then read your prayer each day for a week—or whenever you're feeling down or discouraged.

❧ Psalm 100
❧ Romans 8:28-32
❧ Ephesians 3:20, 21
❧ Psalm 148

_____

_____

_____

_____

March

WEEK 1—Hope Tree

Celebrate the arrival of springtime and hope by planting a family tree. March is a wonderful time for planting! Have your family visit a tree farm or nursery and choose a fast-growing tree to plant in your yard. After the planting, list the hopes you have for the growing tree, such as new leaves, growing taller, bushing out, and blossoms or fruit (if it's a producing tree). Then list hopes for your family, such as better communication, spending fun times together, and praying for each other. Be sure to assess how the tree is growing and how your family hopes are growing every few weeks!

WEEK 2—Help With Hope

As a family, read the following Bible verses to discover the places our hope lies: Philippians 4:13; Psalm 33:20-22; 1 Thessalonians 1:3; 5:8; Titus 1:2; 3:7; and Romans 5:5. Purchase solid-colored placemats and permanent markers. Draw a hope each family member has, then write one of the above verses on each mat. Read the verses at dinner each night for a week, then share a prayer thanking God for giving us powerful hope through Jesus and the Holy Spirit. End by repeating Romans 5:5.

WEEK 3—Hope Grows!

Spring planting is always fun and filled with hope. Have a bit of fun making these happy sponge people and watching them grow as your hope in God grows. Cut sponges into ovals and use permanent markers to draw happy faces on them. Set the sponges in shallow dishes with water, then sprinkle the tops of their "heads" with grass seed. Keep the sponge people in a sunny window and be sure they're spritzed with water each day. As the grassy "hair" begins to grow, explain that hope grows, too. It doesn't sit still but grows because our faith in and love for God continue to grow!

WEEK 4—Sing a Psalm

Have family members form pairs or work in one group to create psalms of thanksgiving for God's love and the hope he brings through the Holy Spirit. See Psalms 89:1, 2, 5; 92:1-5; 96:1-3; and 103:8-18 for ideas. Fit the words to familiar tunes and write the words on a large sheet of paper. Have a family sing-along, then end by repeating Romans 5:3-5. Sing a psalm a day for the next week at dinnertime.

Fun Family Activities

EASTER

PLANTING THE SEEDS

Lilies are blooming, new life abounds, and the joy of Easter is in the air! And though Easter with its vibrant colors and promise of springtime newness is one of our favorite times of year, it certainly was in the beginning one of Christianity's darkest moments. Jesus' death on the eve of that first Easter so long ago brought untold sadness and despair and seemed to freeze the promises God had brought with Christ's ministry. It wasn't until the revelation on the third morning after that believers truly understood the depth of God's Word and Christ's sacrifice. Jesus has risen—Hosanna! Hosanna!

PRE K–K (Romans 5:8b). Very young children adore Easter and all the excitement and colors this springtime celebration brings. It's so important for children to realize that without Jesus there would be no reason for the season! Help young children begin to understand the miraculous love the Lord had for us through the beautiful simplicity of Romans 5:8b. Realizing we're all sinful and need Jesus' love and forgiveness is a big step, and Romans 5:8b is easy enough for young children to remember without being in "over their heads."

ELEMENTARY (Romans 5:8). Kids of all ages love Easter but often tend to focus on the chocolate bunnies, candy eggs, and juicy jelly beans that are as perennial as new grass. Challenge older kids to realize that God didn't just *say* he loves us—he *demonstrated* his love by sending his own Son to die for our sins. Romans 5:8 will give kids a solid basis for why Jesus died and what his death means for us.

YOUTH/ADULT (Romans 5:7, 8). Older youth and adults have heard the Easter story so many times that it may sound almost rote and actually lose some of the meaning, majesty, and miraculous spirit with which it unfolded so many years ago. Bring back the passion and power of the first Easter with Romans 5:7, 8 and help learners realize that God took the ultimate action to *show* his love for us through Jesus' death.

SECRET SCRIPTURE SIGNAL

Each month a new Scripture signal is suggested as a fun way of signaling some-one in your church or family to repeat the month's key verse! For this month's Scripture signal, you'll be making crosses with your fingers. Each time you signal friends or family members with a cross or they signal you, you both must repeat the verse or verses!

GARDENING TIPS

❧ Write the verse or portions of a verse (depending on the age level) on a piece of poster board cut into the shape of a cross. Keep your special cross in a place where you'll see it often!

❧ Each time you see an Easter bunny this month, repeat Romans 5:8 to remember the *real* reason for the season! (There are a lot of bunnies, so get hopping!)

❧ Go on a word search for the phrase "for our sins" in the New Testament to find other verses similar to Romans 5:6-8. What revelations!

WEEK 1—SOWING THE WORD

Photocopy the Fun Family Activities from page 45.

Gather children and explain that this is the time of year for a very special holiday called Easter. Tell children that Easter is the time we celebrate how Jesus rose from the dead after he died for our sins so we could be forgiven by God for disobeying him. Explain that when we disobey God's rules, we sin. And sin keeps us from God and from living with him in heaven.

Teach children the following song based on Romans 5:8. Sing to the tune of "Jesus Loves Me" and perform the accompanying motions with the words.

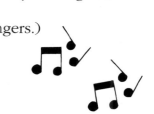

God has shown his love for us (Cover heart with hands.)
Through Jesus dying on the cross— (Make a cross with your fingers.)
While we were still sinners all, (Hang your head.)
Jesus died for one and all. (Make a cross with your fingers.)
While we were sinners, (Hang your head.)
While we were sinners, (Hang your head.)
While we were sinners, (Hang your head.)
Jesus died for us. (Make a cross with your fingers.)

Repeat Romans 5:8b two times and encourage children to repeat the verse with you. End by saying together, "We love and thank you, Jesus. Amen." Hand out the Fun Family Activities.

WEEK 2—KNOWING THE WORD

Before this activity, cut two 6-inch squares of white cotton fabric for each child. You'll need very diluted food coloring, a tub of water, permanent markers, and paintbrushes or cotton swabs.

Sing the Scripture song from Romans 5:8 you learned last week and be sure to do the accompanying motions. Then repeat Romans 5:8b two times aloud. Remind children that God loves us and wanted a way for us to be forgiven from sin. So God sent his Son Jesus to die for us so our sins could be taken away!

Hand out the fabric squares and let children quickly "paint" a few lines or shapes using the diluted food coloring. Tell children the marks stand for the things we say and do that God tells us are wrong. Then explain that when Jesus died for us on the cross, he took away those bad marks so we could live close to God. Dip and swish the fabric in the tub of water and see how the marks disappear. Then hand each child a dry cotton square and help kids draw hearts on the fabric with permanent markers. Tell kids this heart stands for God's love, which will never go away!

End by sharing a prayer thanking Jesus for his forgiveness and God for his love. Then repeat Romans 5:8b once more.

While we were still sinners, Christ died for us. Romans 5:8

WEEK 3—GROWING THE WORD

Before class, cut two 10-inch squares of white tissue paper for each child. You'll also need tape, green chenille wires, and copies of the preschool Scripture Card from page 126.

Lead children in singing the Scripture song for Romans 5:8 that they learned a few weeks ago, then ask children the following questions:

➤ **Who loves us and sent his Son to love us?** (God)

➤ **Jesus died so we can be what?** (forgiven; live with God; live in heaven)

Remind children that because God loves us he sent Jesus to forgive our sins. And because we're forgiven, we can be loving and more forgiving, too. Tell children they'll make love lilies to give to someone they love to remind them how much the Lord loves us.

Have children place two squares of tissue paper on top of each other, pinch the centers of the papers together to make the lilies, then tape the pinched parts to the tops of green chenille wires for the "stems." (Add torn green-paper leaves if you would like.) Tape a Scripture Card of Romans 5:8b to each love lily. End by repeating the verse two times aloud and giving each child a hug of love!

WEEK 4—SHOWING THE WORD

Cut a 12-inch ribbon in each of the following colors for every child: red, white, and black. You'll also need a rubber band for each child to wear on his wrist.

Repeat Romans 5:8b two times aloud, then hand each child a black ribbon. Tell kids this is the color of how we felt before God loved us and sent us Jesus. Then hand out the white ribbons and tell children that white stands for God's pure love. Finally, hand out the red ribbons and explain that this is the color of love because it stands for Jesus dying to forgive us. Sing the Scripture song you learned earlier and wave the color ribbons as you sing.

God has shown his love for us (Wave the white ribbon.)
Through Jesus dying on the cross— (Wave the red ribbon.)
While we were still sinners all, (Wave the black ribbon on the floor.)
Jesus died for one and all. (Wave the red ribbon.)
While we were sinners, (Wave the black ribbon on the floor.)
While we were sinners, (Wave the black ribbon on the floor.)
While we were sinners, (Wave the black ribbon on the floor.)
Jesus died for us. (Wave the red ribbon.)

End by sharing a prayer thanking Jesus for forgiving us and for loving us enough to die for us. Tie the ribbons to the rubber bands for children to wear home.

WEEK 1—SOWING THE WORD

Before this activity, enlarge and photocopy the rebus pictures from page 37 and cut them out. Tape each icon to an index card. You'll also need markers and copies of the Scripture Card for elementary kids from page 127 and the Fun Family Activities from page 45.

Line the Scripture rebus cards on a chalk rail or against the wall. Point to the cards as you repeat Romans 5:8: "But God *(God cloud)* demonstrates his own love *(heart)* for us *(smiles)* in this: *(arrow)* while we were still sinners *(frowns)*, Christ died for us *(cross)*. Romans 5:8."

Explain that this verse tells us not only how great God's love is for us but also how awesome Jesus' love is that he would die for us while we were still sinners. Point out that this is the season for Easter and that we celebrate Jesus' resurrection after his death on the cross for our forgiveness of sins. Invite kids to come point to the pictures in the verse as they repeat the words of Romans 5:8.

Then hand out the Scripture Cards for Romans 5:8 and have kids draw the rebus pictures on the backs of the cards to take home and practice. Give kids the Fun Family Activities to take home. Keep the large rebus cards to use next week.

WEEK 2—KNOWING THE WORD

Cut two 6-inch squares of cotton fabric for each child. You'll also need a tub with water, diluted food coloring, paintbrushes, and permanent makers.

Line up the rebus cards for Romans 5:8 and have kids repeat the verse two times aloud. Then scramble the order of the cards and have a volunteer replace them in the correct order. Continue repeating the process until everyone has had a turn to unscramble the verse. Remind kids that Jesus died to forgive our sins so we could be close to God and live with him in heaven.

Hand each child a square of cloth and have kids use food coloring to paint quick marks on the squares. Have kids think about things they've said or done that God tells us are wrong, then explain that the marks on the cloths represent those things. Then dip the cloths in the water and watch them disappear. Point out that Jesus' death erases our sins when we accept him and are baptized. Then have kids write Romans 5:8 on the dry squares of fabric. Tell kids that these marks will always remain, just as Christ's love is always with us!

But God demonstrates his own love for us in this: While we were still sinners, Christ died for us. Romans 5:8

WEEK 3—GROWING THE WORD

Make a copy of the Scripture Card from page 127 for every four kids. Cut each card into eight pieces and place each set in an envelope.

Ask kids to form groups of four and have each group member repeat Romans 5:8 to her teammates. Then repeat the verse once in unison. Hand out the envelopes containing the Scripture puzzles, then tell groups that each member much choose two puzzle pieces so they can reassemble the verse as a team. When the puzzle is completed, each team is to shout out the verse, then give each other high fives.

With kids still in their groups, have them answer these questions:

❧ **How did God sending Jesus demonstrate his love? How can we demonstrate love to others?**

❧ **In what ways did Jesus' death demonstrate his love for us? his forgiveness of our sins?**

❧ **How can we live in God's love and Jesus' forgiveness? In other words, how do love and forgiveness make our lives different?**

End with a prayer thanking Christ for his sacrifice of love. Then close by repeating Romans 5:8 and saying "amen."

WEEK 4—SHOWING THE WORD

Be sure you have paper, pens, and Bibles. Have kids form small groups and hand each person a sheet of paper and pen or pencil. Hand each group a Bible. Begin by asking each small group to repeat Romans 5:8 together. After each repetition, offer a warm round of applause and appreciation.

Have groups find Romans 5:6-8 in their Bibles. Ask three kids to each read a verse aloud. Then challenge groups to write prayers using some of the words in each of the verses. For example, they might write: "Dear Lord, we know we are sinners and sometimes disobey you, and we know it would be hard to do what Jesus did for us, so we thank you for having Jesus die for us while we were still sinners." Have group members work together on one prayer and each person copy the prayer on his paper. Tell kids they can decorate their prayer pages while waiting for other groups to finish. Then lower the lights or ask for a moment of quiet to set a serious mood. Quietly ask each group to read their prayer, then end each prayer with a corporate "amen."

Challenge kids to pray their prayer of thanks and love each night for the next week, then close their prayer by repeating Romans 5:8.

WEEK 1—SOWING THE WORD

Write Romans 5:7, 8 on a sheet of newsprint or poster board. Write verse 7 on two lines and verse 8 on two lines. Photocopy the Scripture Card from page 128.

Gather learners and have them read Romans 5:7, 8 aloud two times. Then explain that these verses can be learned by lumping the sections as follows:

Very rarely will anyone die for a righteous man,
though for a good man someone might possibly dare to die.
But God demonstrates his own love for us in this:
While we were still sinners, Christ died for us.

Explain that there are four main portions or "lumps" that break these verses down into more manageable parts. Ask participants to tell what the first two lumps teach us and what the last two say. Then hand out the Scripture Cards and have learners underline the lumps as you've done on the newsprint.

Challenge learners to work on either the first two portions or all four at once during the coming week. Suggest they tape the card to a mirror or the dashboard of a car to look at during stoplights. Save the newsprint verses for next week. Hand out the Weekly Word Journals for people to work on during the next few weeks.

WEEK 2—KNOWING THE WORD

Photocopy the Could You? questionnaire, one for every two or three people. Cut apart the verses from last week that were written on the newsprint. Cut each verse into its two portions or lumps. Then place the portions end to end along the chalk rail or ask volunteers to hold them. Invite learners to repeat the verse two times in unison, looking at the verses if they need a helpful hint or two. Then scramble the order of the verse portions and have four volunteers come to rearrange them into the correct order.

Form pairs or trios and hand out the Could You? questionnaires along with pens or pencils. Allow time for discussion, then have learners share their insights with the entire group. End by repeating Romans 5:7, 8 two times, then close by having small groups pray and thank Jesus for his incredible sacrifice of love for our sins.

WEEK 3—GROWING THE WORD

Invite participants to pop up from their seats and each repeat a portion of Romans 5:7, 8. See if you can repeat the verse three times without stumbling over the words! You may wish to go around the room and have each person supply one word of the verses in order. Continue until you've repeated the verse two times.

... But God demonstrates his own love for us in this: While we were still sinners, Christ died for us. Romans 5:7, 8

Form three groups and assign each one of the following portions of Scripture to read: John 10:14-18; John 15:9-14; and 1 John 3:16-24. Then have groups answer the following questions and report their findings to the entire group.

❧ **What should we learn from Jesus' death? What part does love play?**

❧ **How can we pass this knowledge on to others through our words? deeds?**

❧ **How would you summarize your Scripture passage in one sentence?**

Remind participants that Jesus laid down his life for us and for all people for all time. We may not be able to (and hopefully will never have to) lay down our lives for someone, but we can certainly lay down our *love* for all people! End by challenging learners to be more aware of how they treat others this week and by challenging them to lay down their love to others each day.

WEEK 4—SHOWING THE WORD

Have learners greet one another by repeating Romans 5:7, 8, with one person repeating verse 7 and the other verse 8. Go around the room repeating the verse until each person has repeated both verses two times. Remind everyone that God demonstrated his love for us in an amazing way, one that is hard to understand and comprehend totally and certainly not one we'll replicate in our own lives: Christ died for us *while we were still sinners.*

Ask learners how they can respond to such sacrifices as the ones God and his Son made for us. After a few minutes of discussion, form three groups and assign one group Romans 5:6 to read. Have another group read 5:7 and the third read 5:8. Then, using words from each verse, have each group write a portion of a prayer thanking God and Jesus for their sacrifices of love. Tell the group reading verse 6 to begin the prayer with "Dear Lord" and the group reading verse 8 to end the prayer with "amen."

When each group is finished writing, read the prayer aloud. Then close with a moment of silent contemplation for the sacrifice of love made by the Father and Son and the love poured out for us through the Holy Spirit. Challenge learners to repeat Romans 5:7, 8 once a day for a month before their evening prayers.

Could YOU?

1. Verse 7 tells us that not many would—or could—die for someone else. Think hard—could you die for someone in your family? for a complete stranger? for Jesus? Explain your answers.
2. What is our response to Jesus' incredible sacrifice? How does this affect the way we treat others?
3. Verse 8 tells us that Jesus' death was a result of God's love for us. How so? How did God sacrifice for us? How did Jesus sacrifice for us?

April

WEEK 1

God loved Jesus more than anything, yet God chose for *us* to live and for *his own Son* to die.

❧ What does this say about God's love for us?

_____

_____

❧ What new meaning does this give to the phrase, "we're a chosen people"?

_____

_____

❧ How does it make you feel to know that God loves you so much that he allowed his Son to die and you to live?

_____

_____

WEEK 3

Read Romans 3:23; 5:6, 8, 10; and 6:23. We don't like to think about the sin in our own lives—it's much easier to find it in someone else! Honestly answer three "simple" questions.

❧ What are sinful behaviors or attitudes I keep "hidden" from myself and God?

_____

_____

❧ If I had to choose between these behaviors and how God would have me act, which would I choose? Why?

_____

_____

❧ How can I repent from, then change destructive or negative behaviors?

_____

_____

End with a prayer thanking Jesus for his forgiving love and God for his great grace.

WEEK 2

Read 1 John 3:18 and Romans 5:8, then answer these questions.

❧ How does putting love into action demonstrate its sincerity? its outreaching nature?

_____

_____

❧ What have you done in the past day or two to put your own love and caring into action?

_____

_____

❧ Write the names of three people and your plan of action to demonstrate your love to each this week. Write your plans on the back of this paper and refer to them each morning and evening.

_____

_____

WEEK 4

Read Psalm 100 aloud two times. (It's short—and beautiful—so put some passion into it!) Now read Romans 5:6-8 and genuinely feel what God and Christ sacrificed for you personally.

Use the back of this page to write a psalm of deep, heartfelt thanksgiving for the love God has shown you and for all he has given you. Write the psalm in your best handwriting, then read it aloud to the Lord as a *prayerful gift* each day for the next week.

Keep the psalm in your Bible to remind you, whenever you're feeling low, of the unfathomable love God has for you.

April

WEEK 1—Forgiveness Frame

Purchase a small picture frame for each family member. The frames need to be at least 1-inch wide on every side. You'll also need paint pens, glitter glue, and any other craft items you choose for decorating. Have family members take an evening to decorate the frames. Across the top write "I'm sorry." Then turn the frames upside down and write "I forgive you" across the top so the frame can be read either way. Slide a photograph or drawing of each person into this frame. Whenever someone needs to ask forgiveness from a family member, have him present the frame with "I'm sorry" facing up. Then have the person offering forgiveness present her frame with "I forgive you" facing up. Keep the frames in your rooms for several days before returning them to use again. What loving exchanges of family forgiveness you'll discover!

WEEK 3—Stage A Demonstration!

Purchase blank garage-sale signs or make your own by duct-taping a coat hanger or paint stir stick between two pieces of poster board. Make a blank sign for each pair of family members. Read aloud Romans 5:8, then point out that the word *demonstrate* means to show. God showed his love by sending Jesus to pay the price for our sins. Explain that some people carry signs to demonstrate a point they wish to make and that family pairs can make signs to demonstrate their love, praise, and thanks for Jesus. Have pairs decorate signs, then display them in a garden, your backyard, or around the house to remind everyone of the sacrifice of love Jesus made for us.

WEEK 2—Surprise Easter Eggs

Purchase a dozen plastic, pull-apart Easter eggs. Then have family members write words of thanks and praise for Jesus' sacrifice of love on the cross on slips of paper to put in the eggs. (Let young children dictate their words.) In one of the eggs, hide a paper heart with "Romans 5:8" written on it and put a penny inside to represent how Jesus paid for our sins on the cross. Decorate the eggs with permanent markers if you wish. Then have one family member hide the eggs. Go on an egg safari to find the eggs and read the slips of paper aloud. Whoever finds the egg with the penny has to repeat Romans 5:8 aloud and can keep the penny. Replace the slips of paper and put a new penny in the surprise egg. Repeat the happy hunt tomorrow night!

WEEK 4—Rise-n-Shine Treats

Young children love helping with these yummy donut-like treats for breakfast—or anytime! Heat a pan half-filled with vegetable oil. Let kids take apart refrigerator biscuits and pinch them into cross shapes. Gently place each cross in the hot oil (adults do this!) and, when one side is golden brown, turn them over with a fork. When both sides are golden brown, drain the crosses on paper towels, then let kids gently shake the crosses in powdered sugar or cinnamon sugar. Mmm—what a wonderful Easter breakfast treat!

PLANTING THE SEEDS

When you say the word *joy* and match it to a month, May seems to fit the bill perfectly! Not only are they both three letter words ending in the letter *y,* they're synonymous with happiness, laughter, lightness, and celebration. May begins with joyous celebrating on May Day and ends with Memorial Day. What a perfect month to learn Philippians 4:4-7, which is from the New Testament's book of joy!

PRE K–K (Philippians 4:4). Young children are joyous by nature, ready to giggle, smile, and celebrate the everyday joys of life. Sometimes Bible verses can be hard to learn, understand, and remember—but not Philippians 4:4! This joyous verse will have even the youngest children praising God and repeating again and again, "Rejoice!"

ELEMENTARY (Philippians 4:4, 5). Older kids also love Philippians 4:4, 5 because these verses are easy to learn and remember and equally simple to understand and apply. After all, who doesn't catch the light-hearted feel of verse 4 brimming with joy and praise? Let older kids write this simple set of verses, then decorate the papers with symbols of gentleness and joy.

YOUTH/ADULT (Philippians 4:4-7). Youth and adults can always use a bit more light-heartedness and joy to balance the worries and stresses of school, work, families, and other relationships. Philippians 4:4-7 also serves as a powerful reminder of God's grace in giving peace as well as joy in the midst of hectic lives. Break these four verses into two easier-to-learn sets of verses.

SECRET SCRIPTURE SIGNAL

Each month a new Scripture signal is suggested as a fun way of signaling someone in your church or family to repeat the month's key verse! The signal for this month is the word *rejoice.* Each time you or a friend says the word *rejoice,* both of you are to repeat Philippians 4:4. Now go out there and ... rejoice!

GARDENING TIPS

❧ These verses can seem a bit long, but their flow is so natural! Point out how rejoicing leads to a gentle spirit because God is near. And because God is near, we can leave our worries with him knowing he will give us peace through Jesus.

❧ Just for fun, list all words with six or more letters in verses 4-7. Then read the lists and be amazed at the power and comfort you feel!

❧ Have all participants decorate signs that say "Rejoice!" Hang them around church, the home, or in car windows to spread the happiness.

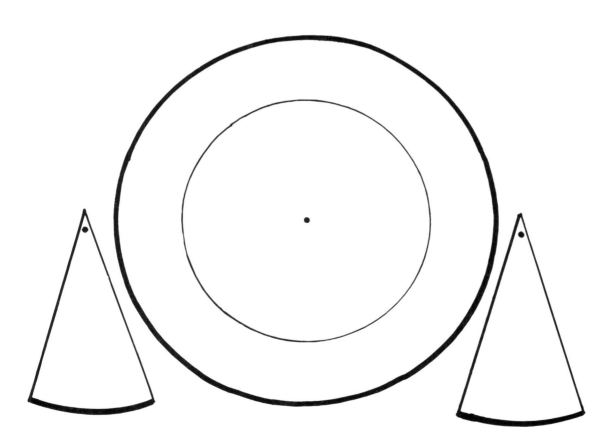

WEEK 1—SOWING THE WORD

Before this activity, blow up and tie off a balloon for each child. Write kids' names on the balloons so there are no mix-ups—and be sure to have a few extras in case a balloon pops! (Tie curling ribbon to the balloons for a more festive feel.) Photocopy the Scripture Card for this age level from page 126. You'll also need tape and copies of the Fun Family Activities from page 55.

Gather children in a circle and repeat Philippians 4:4 to them two times, then encourage children to repeat the verse echo-style with you. Explain that this is a happy verse that teaches us to be glad about God and happy for how much we love him. Point out that springtime is full of happy, bright things that make us feel like singing. Then tell children that God and his love also make us so happy that we want to sing.

Teach children the following song based on Philippians 4:4 and sung to the tune of "Row, Row, Row Your Boat." Sing the song two times without balloons, then sing two more times as children gently bop and bounce their balloons.

Let us rejoice in God;
Let's sing it with our voice.
Then let's sing it all again:
Rejoice! Rejoice! Rejoice!

Let children tape the Scripture Card for Philippians 4:4 to the ribbons on the balloons. Encourage children to practice the verse at home this week and to remember how happy we are to love God each time they look at their happy, festive balloons! Send home the Fun Family Activities.

WEEK 2—KNOWING THE WORD

You'll need large jingle bells for this activity. Large jingle bells or other types of bells can be found at most craft stores.

Have children repeat Philippians 4:4 several times with you. Remind children how joyous we are to love God. Hand out the bells and sing the Scripture song you learned last week as children ring their bells in time to the song.

Explain that Philippians 4:4 tells us to "rejoice in the Lord always." That means we are to praise and joyously celebrate God in every situation, all the time. Play a game in which you name a situation and kids ring their bells and say, "We rejoice in the Lord!" Use some of these situations, then invite children to add their own.

❥ *When we walk outdoors . . .*
❥ *When we wake up in the morning . . .*
❥ *When we're feeling sad and blue . . .*

♪ *When we're playing with our friends . . .*
♪ *When we're not feeling well . . .*
♪ *When we go to bed at night . . .*

Finish by repeating Philippians 4:4 two times aloud. Save the bells to use next week.

WEEK 3—GROWING THE WORD

Cut an 18-inch length of bright ribbon or satin cord for each child. Thread a bell from last week through each ribbon and tie the ends to make necklaces for the children to wear.

Repeat Philippians 4:4 two times, then remind children that we can rejoice in the Lord all the time. In fact, we're so happy to praise the Lord that we want to tell others how much we love him! To help kids do this, explain that you'll play a game of telling others how much you love God. Hand children the bell necklaces to slip over their heads. Then have kids hold their bells silent. Choose one child to start by skipping or hopping to another child and ringing his bell as he says, "I love God!" Then have the other child ring her bell and hop to tell someone else. Keep ringing the bells until all the kids have joyously rung their bells!

End by holding the bells silent and sharing a prayer thanking God for his love and telling him how much you love him, too. Let children wear their bells home as a reminder to rejoice in the Lord all the time.

WEEK 4—SHOWING THE WORD

Begin by singing the Scripture song for Philippians 4:4. Then begin repeating the verse, but stop for children to supply the words at different intervals. Do this several times, then have children give each other joyous high fives for learning God's Word.

Remind children that we feel happy all day and night, no matter what time it is, because we love God. Tell children you'll play a fun game called Tick Tock. Have children sit in a circle on the floor and play this game similarly to Duck, Duck, Goose. Choose one child to go around the circle gently tapping heads and saying, "Tick, tick, tick . . . tock!" On *tock,* the child tapped jumps up to chase the other child back to her starting place. Whoever "wins" must repeat Philippians 4:4. Then the other child becomes the tapper.

Continue until everyone has had a turn to run around the circle, then end by repeating Philippians 4:4 two times. Challenge children to joyously tell God they love him when they wake up in the morning and at night when they go to bed.

WEEK 1—SOWING THE WORD

Enlarge and photocopy the Scripture wheel pattern from page 47 on stiff paper and copy the Scripture Card from page 127 for each child. You'll also need markers, scissors, and brass paper fasteners. Draw the rebus for Philippians 4:4, 5 according to the illustration. Add the words. Tape the poster to the wall.

Gather kids by the poster and have them read the verse silently, then ask for a volunteer to decipher the rebus puzzle and repeat the verses. When the puzzle has been deciphered, have all the kids repeat Philippians 4:4, 5 three times aloud. Explain that this verse teaches us to be happy and gentle because God is with us. Then tell kids they can each make their own rebus Scripture wheels to help learn the verses.

Hand out the Scripture wheels and invite kids to color and cut out the pieces. Show how to attach the pie-shaped pieces to the wheel. Have kids draw the pictures around the wheel and add the reference. The pie-shaped pieces will cover portions of the verses when they're moved around the wheel. Tape the Scripture Cards to the backs of the wheels.

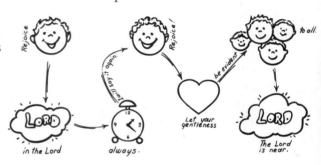

Challenge kids to hide a portion of the verses, then see if they can repeat the missing words. Let kids play this cover-up game with partners.

Put kids' names on the wheels and save them, along with the poster, to use again next week. Hand out the Fun Family Activities.

WEEK 2—KNOWING THE WORD

Cut the rebus Scripture poster from last week into ten pieces. Have kids look at the rebus Scripture wheels they made last week as they repeat Philippians 4:4, 5 two times, then invite pairs of kids to repeat the verses, with one person saying verse 4 and the other verse 5. When everyone has had a turn, ask the following questions. Each time a child answers, have him choose a puzzle piece from the rebus verses and tape it to the wall. (You'll need to ask several children to answer each question.)

❧ **What does it mean to rejoice? How do we rejoice?** (Lead kids to realize that rejoicing comes from the inside and is expressed on the outside.)

❧ **Why are we to rejoice *always*? Does this mean even in hard times? Explain.**

❧ **How is rejoicing a way to show God our love? others our love for God?**

❧ **What is *gentleness*? How does it demonstrate our happiness in God?**

Assemble any missing pieces to the rebus puzzle, then repeat Philippians 4:4, 5 two times aloud. End with a prayer asking for God's help in having a spirit of gladness, joy, and gentleness in all things and in all situations.

Save the puzzle pieces from the rebus Scripture verse to use next week.

Rejoice in the Lord always. I will say it again: Rejoice! Let your gentleness be evident to all.... Philippians 4:4, 5

WEEK 3—GROWING THE WORD

Before this activity, purchase or cut out large white vinyl letters to spell out: "Rejoice! The Lord is near." You'll need a 3-by-4-foot piece of fabric, craft felt, scissors, and tacky craft glue. Shimmery silver, gold, or blue fabric looks lovely for this project! Use colorful permanent markers and glitter glue to decorate the vinyl letters.

Have kids form pairs and hand each pair a rebus puzzle piece. Give kids a few moments to reassemble the verses, then read them aloud once while looking at the puzzle and two times without taking a peek. Give each child a hug for making the effort to learn God's Word and to demonstrate your own joy and gentleness.

Ask kids how they can help others "catch the joy" of loving God. Suggestions might include telling others about God, singing songs, or doing gentle and kind things for others. Explain that today you'll all express your joy in the Lord by making a banner to hang on the wall.

Let kids work together to place and decorate the letters on the fabric and add heart shapes to the banner. When the banner is finished, hang it where everyone will be reminded of the pure happiness we share in the Lord and his love!

WEEK 4—SHOWING THE WORD

Photocopy and enlarge the responsive prayer sentences from this activity. Make a copy for each child and have pens or pencils ready.

Have kids identify the four sections in Philippians 4:4, 5 (each verse has two sentences). Then play a game of Popcorn in which four different kids pop up and each repeat a section of the two verses.

Hand each child a copy of the responsive prayer and a pen or pencil. Have kids fill in the blanks with times when they can rejoice and one way they can express their joy in the Lord, such as through reading the Bible, praying, or singing. When the prayer blanks are filled in, ask for a moment of silence, then have kids take turns reading their prayers aloud. Close by repeating Philippians 4:4, 5 aloud and a corporate "amen." Challenge kids to pray their prayer papers every day during the coming week and to be sure to carry out their plans for rejoicing!

PRAYER TO REJOICE!

Dear Lord, I rejoice in you at all times. When I _____,

I will rejoice in you by _____. And when I

_____, I will rejoice in you by _____.

You alone are Lord, and I rejoice to know you are near!

WEEK 1—SOWING THE WORD

Before this activity, write Philippians 4:4-7 on two sheets of newsprint. Write verses 4 and 5 on one sheet and verses 6 and 7 on another. Tape the pages, one above the other, on the wall or door for everyone to read. You'll also need to photocopy the Weekly Word Journal for May from page 54 for each participant.

Invite learners to read the entire portion of Scripture aloud two times. Explain that these verses teach us about being joyful in the Lord and not spending time worrying. Tell participants that, since this is a longer section of Scripture, you'll be learning the verses two at a time.

Hand a volunteer a pen and ask her to read verses 4 and 5, then underline one time the parts that tell us what we should do. (This includes all of verse 4 and the first part of 5.) Then circle the portion that tells us why we should do this. (This is the second part of verse 5.) Now have a volunteer do the same for verses 6 and 7. (Verse 6 is the "what," and verse 7 is the "why.") Point out that these whats and whys help us to remember the important points of these verses.

Distribute the Weekly Word Journals and encourage learners to work at learning Philippians 4:4-7 during the coming week. Suggest keeping the verses near the sofa or easy chair to look at during television commercials.

Keep the verses on newsprint taped to the wall or door to use next week.

WEEK 2—KNOWING THE WORD

Be sure the verses to Philippians 4:4-7 are still on the wall or door from last week. Have learners repeat all four verses two times aloud, reading from the papers if necessary. Then challenge pairs of learners to repeat verses 4 and 5 without looking at the wall for hints. Have partners help each other if necessary.

Explain that today you'll be looking at verses 4 and 5 and exploring what they mean. Have participants form groups of four or five and discuss the following questions pertaining to Philippians 4:4, 5:

- **What does it mean to rejoice in the Lord? to rejoice always?**
- **How can we rejoice in times of trouble as well as joy?**
- **Who can we show gentleness to and how does this demonstrate love for God?**
- **In what ways does knowing the Lord is near help us rejoice?**
- **What is one way you can rejoice in the Lord today?**

Remind everyone that rejoicing begins in our hearts and spirits and is expressed through our actions and words. End by reading Psalm 100 and repeating Philippians 4:4, 5 two times aloud.

Rejoice in the Lord always. I will say it again: Rejoice! Let your gentleness be evident to all.... Philippians 4:4, 5

WEEK 3—GROWING THE WORD

Hand each person a slip of paper, a small gift bag, and a pen or pencil. Invite learners to repeat Philippians 4:4-7 one time aloud, then ask several volunteers to repeat verses 6 and 7. Use the newsprint verses as needed.

Explain that verse 6 tells us one thing not to do, one thing to do, and three ways to do it. Have learners identify each section and the three ways to give our requests to God (through prayer, petition, and thanksgiving). Point out that *prayer* and *petition* each begin with the letter *p* but that *petition* is second and contains a *t,* which also begins the word *thanksgiving.*

Invite participants to write on their slips of paper requests they wish to make to God. Then have them place the papers in their gift sacks. Explain that trusting God with our requests instead of just senselessly worrying about them is like giving God a gift. And his answers to our requests are like gifts to us! After the papers are in the sacks, repeat verse 7 and discuss how giving our requests to God provides peace and serenity of spirit.

Close by forming a circle and having volunteers pray. Encourage people to ask God to honor your requests and give you peace as you wait for his grace and loving answers to unfold. End with a corporate "amen" and repeat Philippians 4:4-7 one time.

WEEK 4—SHOWING THE WORD

Photocopy a Scripture Card from page 128 for every two or three participants. Cut out the cards, then cut each into six pieces. Mix up the pieces.

Have learners form pairs or trios and sit in groups in a circle. Hand each group six puzzle pieces. Challenge learners to assemble Philippians 4:4-7 by passing and exchanging puzzle pieces with other groups until all their pieces fit together. When a group completes the puzzle, have them repeat the verses. Continue until each group has repeated Philippians 4:4-7.

Form three groups and hand each group a paper and pen. Designate one group the prayer group, one the petition group, and one the thanksgiving group. Explain that each group will write a portion of a psalm or prayer so that when all the portions are read together they will form a wonderful prayer. Allow several minutes for groups to write. Encourage them to use parts of Philippians 4:4-7 (or even include verses 8 and 9).

When all the groups are finished, gather in a group and have each group read its prayer aloud. Begin by saying, "Dear heavenly Father" and end with "In Jesus' name we pray, amen."

Challenge everyone to write a similar prayer to God each night this week. People can give their requests to the Lord and experience the peace that trusting and giving thanks to him brings.

May

WEEK I

Read Philippians 4:4, 5 and Psalm 100, which is an expression of joy. Then consider the following questions:

❥ How does rejoicing demonstrate our love for the Lord? our faith in him?

_____
_____

❥ If you have a joyful spirit, is it possible to be anything other than gentle? Why or why not?

_____
_____

❥ In what ways is gentleness a manifestation of joy, peace, and faith in God?

_____
_____

Write a psalm based on Philippians 4:4, 5 and using Psalm 100 as a model. Read your psalm to someone or present it rolled in a scroll.

WEEK 3

Read Philippians 4:7 twice. On a separate sheet of paper, journal your answers to the following questions. (They're tough, so dig deep!)

❥ God's peace transcends understanding, but how many of our worries also transcend understanding? What does this say about the value of worrying instead of giving worries to God?

❥ If we only accept the logical, is it possible to receive God's peace all the time? Why or why not?

❥ How does peace guard our hearts and minds and keep them in Christ? What else does God's peace do for us?

Write a prayer thanking God for his peace and for helping you have the kind of faith that allows you to go beyond mere logic.

WEEK 2

Zero in on Philippians 4:6, 7 and read these verses two times. Then write your answers to these questions on the back of this page or on a separate sheet of paper.

❥ How can holding on to worries keep you from serving God fully? keep you from being as close to God as possible?

❥ What worries are building a fence around your relationship with God at this moment? (Be honest!)

❥ Verse 6 tells us how to tear down those worrisome fences. Write a three-part plan for tearing down your fences based on prayer, petition, and thanksgiving.

❥ Explain how God's peace transcends understanding. If you can't understand God's peace, what can you do to accept it?

WEEK 4

Divide this section or another sheet of paper in half. On one half, list what Philippians 4:4-7 tells us to do. On the other half, list *why* we're to do these things or what doing these things accomplishes. Read your lists each day this week.

_____
_____
_____
_____
_____
_____
_____
_____
_____
_____
_____

May

WEEK 1—Here and Near!

Gather everyone for a fun evening of shadow-play. Grab a few flashlights and darken the room. Then take turns trying to guess the shadows on the wall. Try categories such as animals, letters, or shapes. Remind everyone that Philippians 4:4, 5 tells us we can rejoice because the Lord is near. Point out that shadows stay with us but that God stays even closer! In fact, God is with us all the time! Fill in the blanks to this poem, then read it every night at dinner or bedtime.

When we _____, God is here; *(something you do)*

When we feel _____, God is near. *(something you feel)*

When we say _____, God always hears us. *(something you say)*

When we're at _____, God stays near us! *(someplace you go)*

WEEK 3—Toss-Across

Use a marker to draw lines on a sheet of poster board, dividing it into four rows of four boxes. In four of the boxes, color a red heart. In four of the other boxes, draw a smile; and in four others, draw a Bible to signify God's Word. Roll two socks together to use as a beanbag. Stand five feet from the game board and toss the beanbag socks. If the socks land on a heart, give another player a hug to show gentleness. If they land on a smile, rejoice and say, "The Lord is near!" If they land on a Bible, repeat Philippians 4:4 or 4, 5. If the socks land on an empty square, toss again!

WEEK 2—Bear Hugs

Purchase inexpensive stuffed bears from a craft store, along with ribbons, lace, glittery fabric, and tacky craft glue. Read Philippians 4:4, 5 and discuss what being gentle means and how a gentle spirit shows love and respect for the Lord. Then invite everyone to make a huggable teddy bear for someone else in the family. Decorate the bears with ribbons, lace, and fabric. Present your gentle teddies and give the recipients warm hugs. Remind everyone that a gentle spirit is like giving God—and others—a warm hug!

WEEK 4—Sweet Dreams!

Purchase a white pillowcase for each family member. You'll also need paint pens or permanent markers. Invite family members to decorate the pillowcases in gentle, restful designs such as hearts, stars, clouds, or rainbows. Remind everyone that Philippians 4:4-7 teaches us to rejoice because God is near—even when we sleep! Plus, we can have peace and comfort knowing God is guarding our hearts and minds in Jesus—even when we're dreaming the night away! Help young children write phrases such as "I love you, God!" or "Jesus is with me" on their pillowcases. Older kids and adults may wish to write all or part of Philippians 4:4-7 on their pillowcases. Sweet dreams!

GOD'S FAMILY

1 Thessalonians 5:9-11

PLANTING THE SEEDS

May and June are months when we celebrate two of the most important family members: mothers and fathers! On Mother's Day and Father's Day we remember all the love we've shared in our families and the powerful part that moms and dads play. Giving guidance when wisdom is weak, kissing scraped knees and bruised egos, and encouraging us through loving words and gentle hugs, moms and dads help us grow into productive, faith-filled adults who can in turn be encouraging and nurturing to our own families. In that vein, 1 Thessalonians 5:9-11 recognizes the importance of encouragement and building one another up not just in our immediate families but in the family of God as well.

PRE K–K (1 Thessalonians 5:11a). Watch young children in a classroom or playground and you'll be surprised how often you hear encouraging words such as "I'll show you," "You can do it," and "You're my friend." You may actually hear these words more often from youngsters than from adults! This month's Scripture, 1 Thessalonians 5:11a, is short but sweet and will be easily remembered with the help of a lively song included in the activities!

ELEMENTARY (1 Thessalonians 5:10, 11). Elementary-aged kids seem to need a big dose of encouragement many times a day. Unsure with so many new things coming their way at school, with relationships, and growing responsibilities in the family, kids need to hear "you're okay" and feel those hugs of encouragement and love often. Help them learn 1 Thessalonians 5:10, 11 by showing kids that careless words and actions can harm as much as loving words and actions can help!

YOUTH/ADULT (1 Thessalonians 5:9-11). Ever notice how youth and adults seem to hold their heads a little higher after a word of praise or encouragement? Perhaps it's because encouraging words and uplifting actions aren't given as freely to this age group as to kids—but they are needed every bit as much! To combat this, use 1 Thessalonians 5:9-11 to remind youth and adults that encouragement and building one another up are part of God's "family plan" and wonderful ways to demonstrate our love for others and for God.

June

SECRET SCRIPTURE SIGNAL

Each month a new Scripture signal is suggested as a fun way of signaling some-one in your church or family to repeat the month's key verse! This month's Scripture signal is an encouraging high five! Each time you give someone a high five, both of you can repeat the verse to help you remember it and to encourage others to learn God's Word, too.

GARDENING TIPS

❥ Write 1 Thessalonians 5:10, 11 on a colorful sheet of poster board and attach it to a wall, door, or bulletin board. Add pictures (and names!) of everyone in your church to this wonderful display of "God's family."

❥ Tape this month's verse to drinking cups or coffee mugs. Repeat the verse each time you take a sip. Remember: God's Word quenches thirsty hearts and spirits!

❥ Make it a habit to repeat the month's key verse first thing in the morning and last thing at night.

WEEK 1—SOWING THE WORD

Before class, photocopy the Fun Family Activities from page 65 for each child.

Give each child a handshake, pat, or hug as you say something encouraging or kind, such as, "I'm so happy you're here" or "You mean a lot to me!" Then tell children that God's Word tells us to be gentle to others and encourage them with kind, helpful words. Explain that when we're kind, encouraging, and helpful to one another we feel filled up (sweep your hands from your feet to high in the air) inside with good thoughts and warm love.

Repeat 1 Thessalonians 5:11a: "Encourage one another and build each other up," then have children repeat the verse two times echo-style. After repeating the verse, have kids find partners and teach them the following action song, sung to the tune of "The Farmer in the Dell," for 1 Thessalonians 5:11.

> ***Encourage one another,*** (Shake partner's hands.)
> ***And build each other up.*** (Pat partner's shoulders.)
> ***Help and share and show you care,*** (Clap hands.)
> ***And God will fill you up!*** (Sweep hands from feet to high in the air.)

Tell children you'll be learning more about encouraging others and being kind in the next few weeks. End by repeating aloud 1 Thessalonians 5:11a two more times. Hand out the Fun Family Activities.

WEEK 2—KNOWING THE WORD

Before this activity, be sure you have plenty of building blocks. You may want to borrow ones from the nursery or gather free blocks and wooden shapes from a building site or lumber yard.

Begin by repeating 1 Thessalonians 5:11a several times aloud, then sing the Scripture song you learned last week to the tune of "The Farmer in the Dell." Remind children that God wants us to be loving and encouraging to other people so they will feel loved. Have everyone give three people a handshake, a gentle pat, or a high five and say, "I'm glad you're here!"

Have children form pairs or trios and hand each small group several blocks. Tell one child in each group to build a nice tower, then prompt the other two to knock it down. Let each have a turn building. Then ask children to tell how it felt to build a nice tower and what it was like to have it torn down. Explain that this is like feeling good, then having someone "tear us down" by being mean or saying ugly things. Point out that it feels better to build things up rather than to tear them down.

End by having children work together to build one large or tall structure, then repeat 1 Thessalonians 5:11a two times and give each other high fives.

Encourage one another and build each other up. 1 Thessalonians 5:11

WEEK 3—GROWING THE WORD

Before this activity, draw the pictures in the margin on construction paper and cut them out for game cards. Make the cards nice and big, then place them in a sack. (While you're making cards this week, you may wish to make extras, since you'll need a card for each child for next week's activity.)

Repeat 1 Thessalonians 5:11a three times aloud, then remind children that God wants us to be kind and encouraging to each other and to make others feel happy and loved. Ask children how they can make others feel happy. Suggestions might include by saying nice things, giving hugs, helping, and sharing.

Have children form pairs. Choose one child to draw a shape from the sack. A heart means give a hug or pat, the smile means say something kind, and the hand means give a high five. Have partners exchange whatever the picture signifies. For example, if the hand is drawn, have partners give each other high fives. You may have to help with what to say when the smile is selected. Suggest statements such as "You're my friend" or "You make me smile." Remind children that these are all ways to encourage and build each other up. Continue until everyone has drawn a picture from the sack. End by singing the Scripture song you learned last week.

WEEK 4—SHOWING THE WORD

If you made extra cards last week with the hand, smile, and heart pictures, all you need now are the Scripture Cards from page 126! If you need to make cards, draw one of the shapes (hand, smile, or heart) on a construction-paper card for each child.

Begin by singing the Scripture song for 1 Thessalonians 5:11a, then give each other handshakes and say "Glad to see you" or "Jesus loves us!" Remind children that kind, encouraging words and deeds make everyone happy—including God! Ask kids who they could hug today or say something kind to this week. Practice being encouraging by sitting in a circle and having one child walk up to someone, give her a pat or handshake, and say, "It's fun being kind—you can be kind, too!" Have the children exchange places and the second child go up to someone else. Continue until everyone has been encouraged and had a chance to encourage someone else.

End by letting children choose a heart, hand, or smile card, then help them tape a Scripture Card to the back. Challenge kids to hand their cards to someone today and then do what the card signifies. Remember: a heart gives a hug, a smile says a kind word, and a hand is for a high five or handshake! Close with a prayer asking God to help you find ways to encourage others. Repeat 1 Thessalonians 5:11a.

WEEK 1—SOWING THE WORD

Enlarge and photocopy the Scripture cards for 1 Thessalonians 5:10, 11 (page 57). Copy one set for each child plus one extra. Color one set of cards and cut them out. Then tape the cards to a sheet of poster board and add the words to the verses as follows: "[cross] He died for us so that, [awake/asleep] whether we are awake or asleep, [people by cross] we may live together with him. [arrow and people with heart] Therefore encourage one another and build each other up, just as in fact you are doing." Tape the Scripture map to the wall. Have fishing line, markers, scissors, tape, drinking straws, and copies of the Fun Family Activities from page 65 ready.

Gather kids in front of the Scripture map and point to the pictures while they repeat the verses twice. Explain that these verses teach us that we're a part of God's family. And family members encourage one another and build each other up. Repeat the verse once more, pointing to the pictures.

Invite kids to make Scripture mobiles. Cut out and decorate the picture cards, then write the corresponding words to the verses on the backs of the cards. Tape varying lengths of fishing line to the cards and suspend them in order from a drinking straw. Challenge kids to hang their mobiles where they can read them often. Give each person a copy of the Fun Family Activities.

WEEK 2—KNOWING THE WORD

Cut out two paper dolls for each child. Seal one paper doll for each child in a peek-proof envelope. Have markers, construction paper, glitter glue, and tape ready. Photocopy the Scripture Card for 1 Thessalonians 5:10, 11 from page 127.

Repeat 1 Thessalonians 5:10, 11 two times aloud, using the Scripture map from last week. Then invite pairs to repeat the verses, with each partner repeating one verse. Lead kids in a round of applause for each pair as a way of encouraging each other. Remind kids that God's Word tells us that we live with Jesus all the time and that since we're all part of his family we're to treat each other in kind, encouraging ways.

Distribute the envelopes containing the paper dolls, but don't tell kids what's inside. Invite kids to tell about times someone said or did something that made them feel bad, such as calling them a name or excluding them from a game. After several learners share, have kids tear their envelopes into five pieces, then pull out what was in the envelopes. When kids see the torn paper dolls, ask:

❥ **What happened to the paper dolls inside?**
❥ **How is this like what can happen if we're not careful with what we say or do to others?**
❥ **Why is it important to build each other up and encourage one another?**

He died for us ... Therefore encourage one another and build each other up.... 1 Thessalonians 5:10, 11

Let kids "build up" the second paper dolls by embellishing them with markers, glitter, and colored paper. Tape the Scripture Cards for 1 Thessalonians 5:10, 11 to the dolls and encourage kids to work on learning God's powerful Word this week.

WEEK 3—GROWING THE WORD

Cut the Scripture map you made earlier into as many puzzle pieces as there are kids. You'll also need cookies, napkins, several cans of fruit juice, and paper cups.

Scramble the Scripture map pictures and set them on the floor. Have kids each take a puzzle piece and work together to reassemble 1 Thessalonians 5:10, 11 as quickly as they can, then lead everyone in repeating the verses aloud.

Remind kids that we're part of God's family and that, as family members, we're to treat each other kindly and be encouraging. Ask:

❥ **In what ways does encouraging others build them up?**

❥ **How can we build each other up through our words? actions? attitudes?**

Explain that you'll set up a snack table after church for anyone who would like to stay for a treat. Ask kids to help you set out the cookies, napkins, juice, and cups. Share a prayer thanking God for being part of his family. Then end by singing the Scripture song below to the tune of "Jesus Loves Me."

Jesus died so we could be part of heaven's family.
We are family of one mind—let's help our family and be kind!
Encourage each other, encourage each other,
Encourage each other, and build each other up.

WEEK 4—SHOWING THE WORD

Write "We'll build 'em up—not tear 'em down! Make a smile—not a frown!" on a sheet of newsprint and tape it to a wall. You'll also need paper and pencils.

Challenge pairs of kids to repeat 1 Thessalonians 5:10, 11. If they need help, let them call on someone to supply the next word. Then hand each pair a piece of paper and a pencil. Invite partners to complete these sentences:

When we _____, we encourage others.
When we _____, we build others up.

For example, kids might write, "When we help and share, we encourage others. When we speak kind words, we build others up." As kids work, have them discuss the value of making others feel valued and built up. After the sentences are written, have each pair read their papers then lead everyone in responding by shouting the rhyming couplet on the newsprint. End with a corporate "amen."

Challenge pairs to do the things they listed during the week and watch for people's reactions. Close by repeating 1 Thessalonians 5:10, 11 two times aloud.

Youth/Adult

WEEK 1—SOWING THE WORD

Write 1 Thessalonians 5:9-11 on a large sheet of newsprint. Leave space between the verses so the Scripture is easier to read. Attach the verses to the wall. You'll need a red marker and copies of the Weekly Word Journal from page 64.

Have everyone read the verses from 1 Thessalonians 5:9-11 one time silently, then read the verses two times aloud. Explain that this month you'll be exploring what God has to say about being part of his family and how we're to treat one another. Point out that each of these three verses states a purpose. Ask learners to identify each purpose and whose purpose it is. (Verse 9 speaks of God's purpose for us to receive salvation; verse 10 tells of Christ's purpose for us to live with him; and verse 11 gives us a purpose in this plan: to encourage others and build them up.) Underline each purpose with the red marker, then draw an arrow to show that verse 9 ends with Jesus and that verse 10 begins with him, and another arrow to show that verse 10 ends with us living "together with" Christ and that verse 11 begins with our responsibility. Explain that God's purpose (salvation) led to Christ's purpose (he died so we can live with him) and that Christ's purpose forms the basis for our own purpose (to encourage and build each other up).

Distribute the Weekly Word Journals and encourage participants to work on learning 1 Thessalonians 5:9-11 during the coming week.

WEEK 2—KNOWING THE WORD

Cut out a paper heart and cloud and seal one of each in an envelope for every three or four people. Cut out an extra heart and cloud for each person.

Have learners repeat 1 Thessalonians 5:9-11 one time, then turn to someone nearby and repeat the verses again. Challenge everyone to be encouraging and give "pats on the back" for learning God's Word so it can be put to work in our lives.

Have people form groups of three or four and distribute the envelopes and a pen to each person. (Don't tell what's in the envelopes!) Direct people to pass the envelopes around, with each person tearing a portion. When everyone has torn an envelope, see if participants can identify what was inside the envelopes, then tell them that the hearts represent our feelings and that the clouds represent our hopes and dreams. Ask groups to discuss these questions:

❧ **How is this activity like saying or doing something that hurts someone?**
❧ **Which is easier: to encourage and build others up or to tear them down? Which better reflects our relationship to God? his family?**
❧ **How can we encourage others? build them up? draw them nearer to God?**

Hand out new paper hearts and clouds and have learners write one way they can encourage someone on the paper heart and one way to build another person up on the cloud. Challenge participants to carry through with their plans during the coming week, then repeat 1 Thessalonians 5:9-11 two times.

For God did not appoint us to suffer wrath ... Therefore encourage one another.... 1 Thessalonians 5:9-11

WEEK 3—GROWING THE WORD

For this activity, you'll need red construction paper, scissors, tape, markers, and several bags of small, wrapped candies.

Invite trios to repeat 1 Thessalonians 5:9-11 aloud. When everyone who wants a turn has had one, end by repeating the verses together. Remind everyone that we're all part of God's family and are to treat others in kind ways through help, caring, speaking encouraging words, and building them up in warm and loving ways. Explain that to encourage God's youngest learners in your church, you'll be making We Care cards to hand out with sweet reminders of how much you care for and support them.

Set construction paper, scissors, markers, tape, and candies on a table. Then encourage learners to cut out construction-paper hearts, write "We Care" across the tops of the hearts, decorate the hearts with lively designs or a short message, then sign their names and tape a piece of candy to each We Care card.

Present the cards after church to kids as they're leaving or as you're sharing in the special surprise they may have made in their own classes! (Check with the elementary class leaders and be sure to give this month's Secret Scripture Signal to several kids to see if they can repeat their verses!)

WEEK 4—SHOWING THE WORD

Cut the verses you wrote on newsprint several weeks ago into as many pieces as there are participants. Have each person take a piece of the puzzle, then work with everyone else to reassemble 1 Thessalonians 5:9-11. Remind everyone to be encouraging and helpful! When the verses are in order, have class members repeat them two times aloud. Then have everyone take a puzzle piece and write his or her name and phone number on the back. Place the pieces in a sack and shake it to mix the pieces. Ask:

- **In what ways can building *others* up build up *ourselves* in Christ?**
- **How can having an encouraging attitude about life draw us closer to God? closer to others? give us peace?**

Remind learners that learning and remembering God's Word is wonderful and something we're commanded to do but that we can't realize its fullness unless we put God's Word into action. Tell participants that they'll have a chance to put 1 Thessalonians 5:9-11 into action—beginning today! Have everyone draw a name from the sack. Whoever they select will be a Build 'Em Up Buddy for the coming week. Challenge buddies to call each other once a day for the next week and chat about how the day went, ask for prayer requests, and be encouraging and kind. (It may be awkward at first, but think of the friendships that may be forged!)

End with a prayer thanking God for helping us be part of his family through Christ and for showing us ways to be encouraging to others.

June

WEEK 1

Read 1 Thessalonians 5:9-11 and think about the three main purposes named in these verses. Write your answers to these questions.

➤ What was God's purpose for us in verse 9? How did his purpose show his love?

_____

_____

➤ What was Jesus' purpose in verse 10? How does it relate to God's purpose in verse 9?

_____

_____

➤ What is our purpose (and responsibility!) in verse 11? How is our purpose related to God's? to Christ's? How does fulfilling this purpose toward others show our love for God and Christ?

_____

_____

WEEK 3

Read 1 Thessalonians 5:11 and Ephesians 4:29-32, then write out your answers to the following questions:

➤ What do these two Scripture passages have in common? How are they different?

_____

_____

➤ How can forgiving others be a way to build them up? build ourselves up through love?

_____

_____

➤ List on the back of this page all the specific ways given in Ephesians 4:29-32 to encourage or build others up. Then circle the ones you regularly demonstrate to others and underline those you need to work on.

WEEK 2

Think about times you've felt hurt or had dreams dashed because of something careless someone said or did. Now think of your own words to others, especially to those in your own family. At times we treat those closest to us carelessly even though they're the most important ones in our lives!

➤ How does building up our families help us stay close to one another? close to God as a family unit?

_____

_____

➤ How does encouraging family members show them that they're important? demonstrate your love for them?

_____

_____

➤ In what specific ways can you encourage each family member's hopes and dreams? faith?

_____

_____

WEEK 4

Read Psalm 46. Do you feel uplifted and encouraged? What a beautiful psalm to calm the heart, stir the soul, and renew our faith and strength in the mighty God we serve!

Read the psalm once more, but this time write down on the back of this page or underline in your Bible each line that encourages or builds you up. (You may end up writing the entire psalm!)

Now commit to reading this beautiful psalm each night for the next week before thanking God for his own loving encouragement in your life!

June

WEEK 1—Family Ties

Let each family member prepare a note bag to use in the coming weeks. Place the following items in a self-sealing sandwich bag: index cards or pieces of white paper, construction paper, several markers, and as many 6-inch pieces of ribbon as there are papers. Encourage everyone to write or draw encouraging messages to secretly tie to other family members' doors or bedposts. For added fun, leave notes in other places where they will be discovered and delightfully enjoyed!

WEEK 2—Towering Encouragement

Play a game similar to a game played in many countries where players build huge towers out of cards, blocks, or other materials until they tumble down. Use playing cards, blocks, or sugar cubes and have players take turns telling ways to encourage others, such as through prayer, helping, speaking kindly, or being good listeners. Add one piece to the tower each time you name a way to encourage or build someone up—or add each word to a Scripture verse review. When the tower tumbles, give high fives and begin again!

WEEK 3—Build 'Em Up Burritos

Prepare this yummy family snack feast as you review how building others up makes everyone feel. Set out flour tortillas, refried beans, cheese, shredded lettuce, chopped tomatoes, and picante sauce. (If you're serving this for a meal, you may wish to add seasoned ground beef, too.) Let everyone name a way to encourage others as he or she adds an ingredient to the burritos. Point out that the more we encourage and build others up, the better they feel—just like when you add lots of delicious ingredients to the burritos. Repeat 1 Thessalonians 5:11 before nibbling your goodies.

WEEK 4—Long-Distance Encouragement

Have your family write letters and draw pictures to encourage someone far away. You may decide to encourage grandparents living in another city or even church-sponsored missionaries in another country. Be sure to add a decorated card with 1 Thessalonians 5:11 written out on it. Then send your long-distance encouragement off with a prayer for that person.

LOYALTY TO GOD
1 Corinthians 8:5, 6

PLANTING THE SEEDS

In July our thoughts often turn to the issue of loyalty as the Fourth of July kicks off the month with a raucous celebration of freedom and national pride. Many countries in the world don't share our freedoms and are forced to follow one master or leader even though it may not be what they desire. But Christians all over the world understand that there is a much higher freedom and ultimate master to love, serve, and remain loyal to! In 1 Corinthians 8:5, 6 we learn that we serve and are loyal to one God, the Father, through one Lord, Jesus Christ. What a wonderful portion of Scripture to learn this month as we celebrate the freedom that only Christ can bring!

PRE K–K (1 Corinthians 8:6). Young children are just beginning to realize what the concept of loyalty means and how to be loyal to parents, siblings, and their first friends. What a great verse to teach about the oneness of God and Christ and how all we do is for God. Shortened portions of 1 Corinthians 8:6 have been chosen to learn, but the entirety of verse 6 is presented through a catchy finger rhyme.

ELEMENTARY (1 Corinthians 8:6). The repetition within 1 Corinthians 8:6 will make learning the verse enjoyable and easy for older kids. Elementary-aged kids will understand the concept of oneness and the importance of serving, loving, and praising God through Jesus. These kids will also begin to understand the unique difference between the words *for, from,* and *through* and how they apply to this verse and our relationships with God.

YOUTH/ADULT (1 Corinthians 8:5, 6). Youth and adults often have their focus on things and people other than the Lord. They do not do this on purpose, but because school, jobs, money, and relationships are so central to their lives. Thus, 1 Corinthians 8:5, 6 is a needed reminder that God reigns supreme and that through Christ we receive love, forgiveness, blessings, and much more. Help this intense, "otherwise occupied" group refocus their purpose and praise on the one master we're to serve—God!

SECRET SCRIPTURE SIGNAL

Each month a new Scripture signal is suggested as a fun way of signaling someone in your church or family to repeat the month's key verse! This month hold up one finger as a symbol for the number one. Each time you or someone else gives the secret signal, repeat the key verse.

GARDENING TIPS

❯ Since 1 Corinthians 8:6 is a relatively easy verse to remember, consider having older elementary kids work on verse 5 as well.

❯ Help everyone remember that these powerful "oneness" verses come from *First* Corinthians, not *Second* Corinthians!

❯ Lead elementary kids to understand the difference between "from" and "through" by giving the example of being *from* your town as opposed to going *through* it.

WEEK 1—SOWING THE WORD

Copy the circular icons from page 67 on stiff paper, one for each child. Tape a paper loop on the back of each circle so children can wear them as rings. You'll use the icons to learn the verse today and the finger rhyme next week. Make a complete set of finger icons of your own. Children will be learning only portions of 1 Corinthians 8:6, but they'll learn a bit more through the finger rhyme. This week you'll need these finger icons: the number one, the symbol for God, and the cross. You'll also need one copy of the Fun Family Activities from page 75 for each child.

Slide the icons on your fingers in the order given above. Repeat the following portions of 1 Corinthians 8:6:

> ***"There is but one God, the Father . . .*** (Move the number one and God icons.)
> ***and there is but one Lord, Jesus Christ."*** (Move the number one and cross icons.)

Tell children this verse teaches us that there is only one God and one Lord Jesus. Remind children that God made all things and that we love God and Jesus with all our hearts! Then hand out the same icons to the children and have them slip the icons on their fingers. Slowly repeat the verse three times as children follow along moving their icons. Then play a quick identification game. Ask:

❧ **Who made the world?** (Wiggle the God icon.)
❧ **Who's our best friend who loves us all the time?** (Wiggle the cross icon.)

Finish by repeating 1 Corinthians 8:6 two more times, then distribute the Fun Family Activities. Keep the icons to use again next week.

WEEK 2—KNOWING THE WORD

Be sure you have the icons from last week ready. You'll need a complete set of icons for each person, including yourself.

Slip the icons for 1 Corinthians 8:6 on your fingers as you did last week and repeat the verse two times with the children echoing your words. Then slide on all the icons in this order: the number one, the symbol for God, the world, the people, and the cross. Have children slip the matching icons on their fingers. Then teach children the following finger rhyme as they waggle each icon at the appropriate time.

> ***There is but one God—*** (Move the number one and God icons.)
> ***No, not two!***
> ***Who made the world and me and you!*** (Move the world and people icons.)
> ***There is but one Lord, and Jesus is his name;*** (Move the number one and cross icons.)
> ***And just like God, he loves us all the same!*** (Move the God and people icons.)

Remind children that God made the world and each of us and that Jesus loves us, just as God does. Close by repeating 1 Corinthians 8:6 and having children move their finger icons. Let children take their finger icons home to practice the verse.

WEEK 3—GROWING THE WORD

Before you begin, make a paper-plate icon of the number one for each child. Make the number ones big, bold, and colorful! Scatter and tape the paper-plate icons to the floor.

Have children choose a paper plate to stand beside. Repeat 1 Corinthians 8:6, then let children take turns hopping on and off the number one icons as you repeat the verse aloud three more times. Invite children to sit on the paper plates, then ask:
- ❧ **How many gods are there?** (Just one!)
- ❧ **How many lords are there?** (One, Jesus Christ)
- ❧ **Who is the Father?** (God)
- ❧ **Who is our Lord?** (Jesus!)

Have children repeat the rhyme you learned last week as they hop on and off the number one icons. Then tell children to hang their paper plates on a wall so each time they see the big number ones, they'll remember that there's only one God and only one Lord Jesus.

WEEK 4—SHOWING THE WORD

Cut large number ones from colored poster board. Be sure these numerals are at least five inches wide and ten to twelve inches high. Supply a variety of craft items with which to embellish the numerals, such as glitter glue, sequins, bingo daubers, craft glue, markers, crayons, and even buttons. You'll also need copies of the preschool Scripture Card for 1 Corinthians 8:6 from page 126.

Cover a table with newspapers and have children sit around the table. Hand each child a large number one and hold them high as you repeat 1 Corinthians 8:6 two times. Then tell children they'll decorate their large number ones to remind them that there's only one God, who is the Father, and one Lord, Jesus Christ!

Let children decorate their numbers, then glue Scripture Cards to the backs of the festive numerals. Tell children to keep their number ones where they'll see them often and to ask a family member to read the Scripture Card on the back as they recite the verse. Close by sharing a prayer thanking God and Jesus for being number one in your lives.

WEEK 1—SOWING THE WORD

Write the words to 1 Corinthians 8:6 on a large sheet of poster board. Write the verse in four lines, starting new lines after "Father," "live," and "Christ." Tape the Scripture poster to the wall or door for kids to see. You'll also need pens or pencils and a copy of the Scripture Card from page 127 and Fun Family Activities from page 75 for each child.

Distribute the Scripture Cards, then gather kids by the Scripture poster and read the verse two times aloud. Ask kids to identify any common parts or words in the different lines of the verse, then circle the common words on the poster and on the Scripture Cards. Tell kids that this verse reminds us that there's only one God, who is the Father, and only one Lord, Jesus Christ.

Have kids form pairs and see if partners can help each other learn this verse in a few minutes. Then challenge partners to repeat the verse together with only two helps from others. Lead kids in lively applause for each pair.

End by having kids take their Scripture Cards home to practice during the week. Distribute the Fun Family Activities for July. Keep the Scripture poster to use next week.

WEEK 2—KNOWING THE WORD

You'll need three index cards and a marker for each child. Be sure the Scripture poster from last week is in place and gather kids around it. Repeat 1 Corinthians 8:6 two times aloud, then invite kids to repeat the verse without looking if they can.

Ask kids to look at the verse and remind them you already circled the common words in the verse. Now underline the words *from* and *for* in the second line and both occurrences of *through* in the fourth line. Ask:

- ❧ **What's the difference between being *from* someone and being *through* someone?** (God made everything, and all things come *from* him, whereas things such as forgiveness, love, mercy, and everlasting life come *through* Jesus.)

- ❧ **What's the difference between living *for* someone and living *through* someone?** (When we live *for* God, everything we do is *for* him—we serve for God, we love for God, we share for God, and so on. Jesus helps us do these things so it is *through* Jesus that we serve *for* God or love others *through* Jesus *for* God.)

Have kids write the words *for, from,* and *through* on three index cards. Then repeat 1 Corinthians 8:6 again, having kids hold up the words in the right places.

End with a prayer thanking Jesus for helping us live *for* God *through* him.

Yet for us there is but one God, the Father, ... and there is but one Lord, Jesus Christ.... 1 Corinthians 8:6

WEEK 3—GROWING THE WORD

Practice folding and cutting out three linked hearts from 18-inch lengths of white shelf paper. Cut an 18-inch length of paper for each child. You'll also need scissors, markers, tape, and copies of the Scripture Card from page 127.

Invite kids to form pairs and have each pair repeat 1 Corinthians 8:6 together. After each repetition, have partners give each other high fives. Remind kids that whatever we do, we are to do it *for* God *through* Jesus' loving help and guidance.

Hand each child a length of paper and demonstrate how to fold and cut the paper into the linked hearts. Have kids think of three things they want to do for God this week, such as help someone, read the Bible each night, or learn another verse. Write one way across the top of each heart, then use markers to decorate the lower portions of the hearts. Point out how these hearts have holes so things can go through them to remind us how everything we do for God goes through Jesus. Tape the Scripture Card somewhere on the hearts and have kids read the verse aloud to two other people.

Challenge kids to pray each day for Jesus' help to do the things listed on the hearts. Share a prayer thanking God and Jesus for being number one in your lives.

Fold here.

WEEK 4—SHOWING THE WORD

Cut the Scripture poster into ten pieces. Place the pieces on the floor beside the door and a roll of tape by the pieces.

Have kids sit in a circle and go around the circle having each person supply one word from 1 Corinthians 8:6. See if you can make it through three times with no mistakes! Remind kids that whatever we do for God, we do it through Jesus. Tell kids you'll play a game to review 1 Corinthians 8:6. Have kids form three teams. Explain that when you give a word, such as *help*, the first person to hop up and say, "We help for God through Jesus!" can choose a puzzle piece and tape it to the door. Remind kids to use this pattern for answering: **We** (blank) **for God through Jesus.** Use the following words or phrases, then make up more of your own:

- serve others
- love
- show obedience
- learn about the Bible
- worship
- respect others

When the verse is reassembled, have kid repeat it together. Close by reading Psalm 100 and sharing a prayer praising God for being our heavenly Father and Jesus for being our Savior and forgiver. Challenge kids to remember that all they do is *for* God and is accomplished *through* Jesus!

WEEK 1—SOWING THE WORD

Write 1 Corinthians 8:5, 6 on a large sheet of poster board. Write verse 5 on the top half of the poster and verse 6 on the lower half. Attach the poster to the wall. Keep a red marker handy, as well as pens or pencils. Photocopy the Scripture Card from page 128 and the Weekly Word Journal for July from page 74 for each person.

Have everyone read 1 Corinthians 8:5, 6 two times aloud, then look for patterns in the words and phrases. Explain that these verses teach about the oneness of God and Jesus and contain a wonderful surprise that is often overlooked by people learning these verses. Tell them you'll discover the surprise next week.

Hand out the Scripture Cards. Invite participants to identify any patterns they see in the verses, such as words common to both halves of verse 6. Write any contrasting or shared words beside the verses on the poster board and on the Scripture Cards. For example, write the words *many* and *one* to show that verse 5 talks about many gods while verse 6 mentions one God and one Lord. Write the words *from, for,* and *through* to highlight the differences and similarities within verse 6. Have learners associate the name *God* with the words *from* and *for* and the name *Jesus* with both occurrences of *through* in verse 6.

Challenge learners to picture these patterns and words in their minds as you repeat 1 Corinthians 8:5, 6 three times aloud. Suggest that learners put the Scripture Cards beside their placemats on the table to read at the start and close of each meal. Hand out the Weekly Word Journals. Keep the Scripture poster to use in the coming weeks.

WEEK 2—KNOWING THE WORD

Have everyone look at the Scripture poster and repeat 1 Corinthians 8:5, 6 two times aloud. Remind everyone that there's only one God and one Lord in our lives. Then explain that you'll reveal several important differences found in verse 6. Point out that at first glance this verse sounds repetitive—as though it contains the same words—but that there are really striking differences that change the meaning. Ask:

- **What's the difference between the phrases "from God" and "through Jesus" in verse 6?** (God made everything and all things come *from* him, whereas forgiveness, love, mercy, and everlasting life come *through* Jesus.)
- **What's the difference between the phrases "for God" and "through Jesus" in verse 6?** (When we live *for* God, everything we do is focused on his will and on him. Because Jesus helps us accomplish these things, we love *through* Jesus *for* God or serve *through* Jesus *for* God.)
- **How do these differences change the way you live and respond to God and others? In what way do these differences define the gifts God and Jesus offer us?**

End by sharing a prayer thanking God for being our focus and our purpose in life and Jesus for helping us live and accomplish God's will through him.

... There is but one Lord, Jesus Christ, through whom all things came and through whom we live. I Corinthians 8:5, 6

WEEK 3—GROWING THE WORD

Challenge learners to review the patterns and differences in 1 Corinthians 8:5, 6, including *many, one, one* in verse 5 as well as the differences between *from* and *through* and *for* and *through* in verse 6. Remind everyone that we serve only one God and one Lord and that what we do *for* God is accomplished *through* Jesus. Then have learners form small groups to answer the following questions:

- ✦ **What "gods" and "lords" do you think verse 5 is talking about?**
- ✦ **What "lords" or "gods" that we're unaware of might we serve in our lives?** (Suggestions might include money, jobs, popularity, or looks.)
- ✦ **What does Matthew 6:24 say about serving more than one master?**
- ✦ **How can you be sure that you serve only one God and one Lord?**

End by having each small group pray for guidance in serving only God and Christ each day and helping us identify false gods who threaten our time and focus away from the real God.

WEEK 4—SHOWING THE WORD

Photocopy the Scripture Card for 1 Corinthians 8:5, 6 from page 128 and the question box from this activity, one for every three people. Cut each Scripture Card in three distinctive pieces so participants can put the puzzles together easily.

Repeat 1 Corinthians 8:5, 6, then point out that verse 6 begins with the words "yet for us." Remind everyone that, although others might live for worldly gain, we live for God through Jesus. Invite learners to form trios by matching up the pieces of their Scripture Cards. Hand out the question boxes and instruct trios to follow the directions. After several minutes, have trios read their prayer lines and close with a corporate "amen."

Read 1 Corinthians 12:4-6 and Ephesians 4:4, then answer these questions.

- ✦ What does 1 Corinthians 12:4-6 tells us about the oneness of God and the nature of the Trinity? How do all work for one purpose?
- ✦ Ephesians 4:4 talks about one hope, one faith, and one baptism. What other "ones" do we have in God and in Christ?
- ✦ Write a rhyming two-line prayer based on 1 Corinthians 8:5, 6 by filling in missing words to these lines.

> O Lord, we praise you for _____;
>
> In our lives you reign number one—
>
> We will continually _____,
>
> Through our Savior, Jesus your Son! Amen.

July

WEEK 1

Read Matthew 6:24, then answer these questions about serving God.

❧ Why isn't it possible to serve two masters?

_____

_____

❧ How does 1 Corinthians 8:5, 6 define the master we serve? define how we serve?

_____

_____

❧ List three ways you can serve God through Christ this week.

_____

_____

_____

WEEK 2

Read 1 Corinthians 8:6 and think about the differences between *from* and *through*. Then answer these questions.

❧ In what ways do *all things* come from God? through Jesus?

_____

_____

❧ Verse 6 says we live through Jesus. What are three specific things we do *through* Jesus?

_____

_____

❧ Name two ways you can go through Jesus to reach God with your love this week.

_____

_____

WEEK 3

The early Israelites did not have Jesus to go through to take their love, praise, and sins to God. Read Hebrews 5:1-3; 7:23-28; 9:1-7, 23-28 then answer these questions.

❧ How did the early Israelites "reach" God? Who was their "go-between"?

_____

_____

❧ In what ways did Jesus change this? How did Jesus bring us closer to God?

_____

_____

❧ What did the curtain in the temple signify?

_____

_____

❧ When the curtain tore at the moment of Jesus' death, how did this show the beginning of what 1 Corinthians 8:6 teaches?

_____

_____

WEEK 4

Titus 2:14 states that we are a "peculiar people" (KJV), while 1 Corinthians 8:6 says "yet for us," intimating that we're set apart from others.

❧ In what other ways are we a "peculiar people"—that is, different from people who don't know or love Jesus?

_____

_____

❧ Why do you believe God calls us to be his chosen people, different from the world?

_____

_____

❧ How can you explain to others that you live *through* Jesus *for* God?

_____

_____

❧ On the back, write a paragraph defining who you are *through* Jesus and *for* God.

July

WEEK 1—Apple Routing

Make simple apple crisp by pouring a can of applesauce into a bowl and stirring in a tablespoon of cinnamon. Top with brown sugar and granola. Heat in a microwave for three minutes until warmed through. As you enjoy your treat, talk about the route the apples took to get to you. For example, the apples started in an orchard, but went through pickers, boxers, shippers, and the store. Point out that all things begin with God but that he sends us love, forgiveness, and much more through Jesus! End by repeating 1 Corinthians 8:6 and thanking God for his special routing path—Jesus!

WEEK 3—Scripture Cards

Write the words for 1 Corinthians 8:6 on index cards, one word per card. Make two sets. Use your Scripture Cards to play the following games.

❧ *Scripture Concentration*—Shuffle the cards and place them face down. Take turns turning over the cards and matching words. If you don't make a match, turn the cards face down again, but remember where they are! Continue until you've matched all the words.

❧ *Scripture Fishing*—Scramble the cards face down. Have each player choose three cards. Take turns asking other players if they have one of the words you have. If a match is made, place the pair on the table. If no match is made, the next player goes fishing. Continue until someone is out of cards.

❧ *Scripture Old Maid*—Add an index card with a funny face. Shuffle and deal out all the cards. Choose a card from another player. If they match, lay down the pair. The person stuck with the funny face is the Old Maid.

WEEK 2—Only One!

Have family members form pairs or trios and each decide on a category you might find pictures for in magazines, such as foods, clothing, toys, or cars. Tear out the pictures and tape them to large sheets of paper as collages. After you're done, show each other your handiwork and chat about how there are many types of earthly things, including houses, plants, and people, but only one God, who is the Father, and one Lord, Jesus. Repeat 1 Corinthians 8:6 and write the words "one God" and "one Lord" on another sheet of paper. Hang your pictures where you'll see them often and be reminded there's only God and Savior whom we love!

WEEK 4—Two-Way Street

Form two family teams. Have one team draw pictures of what comes from God while the other group draws what comes through Jesus. Compare the two picture posters, then discuss how God sends love, forgiveness, mercy, and help through Jesus and how we send our love, praise, and service to God through Jesus. Point out that Jesus is like a two-way street where all things come through him to God and from God to us! Write the first part of 1 Corinthians 8:6 on the God poster and the second half on the Jesus poster.

Fun Family Activities

GOD'S PRESENCE

Joshua 1:8, 9

PLANTING THE SEEDS

Comfort. What does it mean to you? A cool fan on a sultry summer day? Maybe a soft blanket and bed when you're not feeling well or a hug from your favorite hug-giver. Comfort comes in many shapes and sizes but none so awe-inspiring, peace-producing, or love-filled than the comfort we receive in knowing that God is always with us and that his Word is alive in our lives. And the best part? God *promises* to be with us—no matter what, no matter when, and no matter where!

PRE K–K (Joshua 1:9b). Young children become unnerved and nervous about a host of things from thunder and lightning to being left "alone" at school or the baby-sitter's house. They know the comfort that the presence of loved ones such as mommy, daddy, and grandparents brings. Now is a wonderful time for your youngsters to discover that God is always with them—even when loved ones step out for an evening. Joshua 1:9 is simple enough for any preschooler to remember but powerful enough to give them something to cling to.

ELEMENTARY (Joshua 1:9). Older kids aren't as timid as they were when they were younger, and they are beginning to assert—and enjoy—their growing sense of independence and autonomy. But they still derive great comfort and security in knowing that God is with us all the time. Kids are also discovering that God's continual presence affects their choices in life, from choosing their friends to what they do in their spare time. Joshua 1:9 reinforces the fact that God is present in our lives and his Word is alive in our hearts.

YOUTH/ADULT (Joshua 1:8, 9). Why is it that many adults and older teens think they can hide from God or ignore his presence in their lives? Maybe the issue of control rears its head, or perhaps a bit too much confidence comes with age and reliance seeps away. But in the midst of feelings that everything is under control, feelings of discouragement, worry, and the need to rely on someone older and wiser are often tucked away. Joshua 1:8, 9 reminds teens and adults that God is in control, that he is present in all situations and places, and that his Word is a solid foundation for success, prosperity, and strength.

SECRET SCRIPTURE SIGNAL

Each month a new Scripture signal is suggested as a fun way of signaling some-one in your church or family to repeat the month's key verse! For this month's Scripture signal, you'll clap two times. Each time you or a friend claps two times, you can both repeat the verse. What a great way to follow the Leader!

GARDENING TIPS

❥ Teens and adults may wish to use the 1-2-2-1 pattern for Joshua 1:9 that the elementary kids are learning: 1 question-command; 2 things to do (be strong and courageous); 2 things not to do (be terrified or discouraged); and 1 promise (God will be with us).

❥ Make a Scripture poster from a 10-foot length of white shelf paper that has the words to Joshua 1:9 written across it. Let church members and family mem-bers sign the poster to show they know God is with them. Display the poster in a place where it will be seen and remembered often.

❥ If you have a family outing or church picnic this August, be sure to play a rousing game of Follow the Leader and encourage even the adults to join in the fun. Remind everyone that God follows us and is with us wherever we go—even down the playground slides!

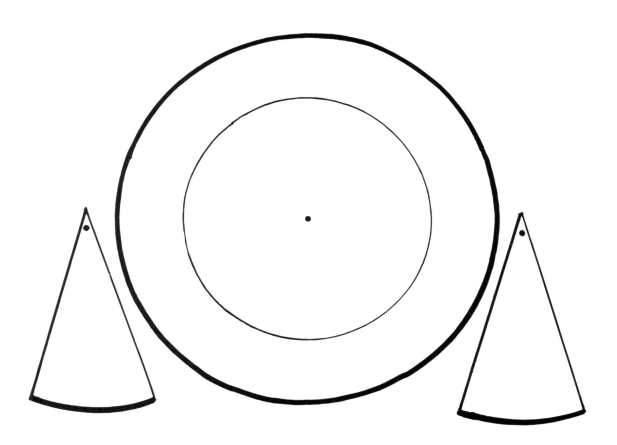

WEEK 1—SOWING THE WORD

Before this activity, photocopy the Fun Family Activities from page 85.

Greet children warmly and tell them you're glad they're here. Then tell kids they'll be learning what the Bible says about God being with us all the time and every place. Teach children the following action rhyme based on Joshua 1:9b. Say the rhyme in a snappy rhythm and lead children in the specified actions.

> *Wave your hands to and fro;*
> *God will be with you wherever you go!*
> *Hop-hop fast, tiptoe slow;*
> *God will be with you wherever you go!*

After children are familiar with the words and rhythm, try substituting new actions such as "sway your body to and fro" and "spin around fast, clap your hands slow." Then ask children to sit in a circle and explain that God is always with us wherever we go and that God stays with us because he loves us.

Repeat Joshua 1:9b several times, having children echo the verse after you. End by distributing the Fun Family Activities.

WEEK 2—KNOWING THE WORD

Before starting, cut out a pair of large, black "shadow" hearts for each child. Have tape handy.

Invite children to sing the action rhyme based on Joshua 1:9b that you learned last week. Challenge children to add new actions, then end by repeating Joshua 1:9b two times aloud.

Remind children that God is with us all the time and wherever we go. Then ask children: What is black and fun and with us in the sun? After kids offer their ideas, tell kids the answer is a shadow! Then help children tape the shadow hearts to the backs of their shoes so the shadows follow them when they walk. Explain that these special shadows remind us of God's love, which is with us wherever we go. Invite children to name places God is with us, such as at home, at church, at the park, or while we're sleeping in bed. Each time a place is mentioned, repeat Joshua 1:9b and skip or hop in a circle.

End by repeating Joshua 1:9b two times and telling children to wear their shadows home to remind them that God and his love are always with us.

WEEK 3—GROWING THE WORD

You'll need a colorful sticker for each child. You may wish to use "Jesus loves me" stickers or colorful heart stickers.

Have children repeat Joshua 1:9b with you three times. Then praise children for trying so hard to learn God's Word and tell them how happy God is to hear them repeat his Word. Hand each child a sticker to place on the back of her hand. Have children hop to one end of the room, then tiptoe to the other side. Let them crawl under a table and over a chair. Then ask if the stickers are still with them. Explain that just as the stickers stay with them wherever they go, God is with us wherever we go. Point out that God never leaves us, so we never have to feel alone or afraid. Then name times when God is with us, such as during storms or when we're away from family members. Have kids respond to each time named by saying "God is with us!" and holding their hands with the stickers high in the air. End by sharing a prayer thanking God for being with us all the time and every place.

WEEK 4—SHOWING THE WORD

Before this activity, collect four large beads for each child: white, red, yellow, and black. You'll also need thick elastic cord. Cut the cord into one 6-inch length for each child.

Review Joshua 1:9b by repeating the action rhyme you learned the first week. Repeat the rhyme several times, changing the actions. Then have kids say Joshua 1:9b two times aloud and end with a cheer that God is always near!

Remind children that God is with us, loving us all the time wherever we go. Hold up a white bead and tell children that this white bead reminds us of God's purity and power. Explain that the red bead stands for God's love, which is with us wherever we go. The yellow and black beads stand for day and night because God is with us all the time.

Then help children use the elastic cord and the beads to string bracelets. Tie the ends of the cord when the beads are strung and let children slip the bracelets on their wrists. Repeat Joshua 1:9b as you point in order to the white, red, yellow, and black beads. Challenge children to wear their bracelets all day and wherever they go to remind them that, just as the bracelets stay with them, God is with them wherever they go.

WEEK 1—SOWING THE WORD

Before this activity, enlarge and photocopy on stiff paper the Scripture wheel from page 77 and the Fun Family Activities from page 85. The Scripture wheel should be about the size of a paper plate and the wedge an appropriate size to match the wheel. Have scissors, markers, and brass paper fasteners ready. You'll also want to write Joshua 1:9 on a sheet of newsprint and tape it to a wall or door for kids to read.

Gather kids by the verse on the wall and have them read the verse aloud two times with you. Explain that this verse teaches us that God never leaves us alone and that we can be brave and hopeful because God is with us all the time. Point out that the verse begins with a question. Have children repeat the verse twice.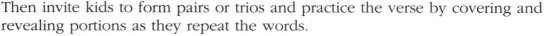

Hand out the Scripture wheels and let kids color the wedge and wheel and write the verse in small letters around the wheel. Show kids how to attach the wedge to the center of the wheel with a brass paper fastener. Then invite kids to form pairs or trios and practice the verse by covering and revealing portions as they repeat the words.

Have kids take their Scripture wheels home to practice. Hand out the Fun Family Activities to complete with their families this week.

WEEK 2—KNOWING THE WORD

Be sure the Joshua 1:9 poster is still on the wall. You'll also need colored markers. Photocopy the Scripture Card on page 127.

Have kids look at the verse as they repeat it one time. Then challenge pairs of kids to repeat the verse without looking, unless they need help. Lead kids in a lively round of applause after each repetition. Remind kids that because God is with us wherever we go, we never have to be afraid or feel alone.

Point out that there's a 1-2-2-1 pattern in Joshua 1:9:

- *one question:* **"Have I not commanded you?"**
- *two things to be:* **"Be strong and courageous."**
- *two things not to be:* **"Do not be terrified; do not be discouraged,"**
- *one promise:* **"for the Lord your God will be with you wherever you go."**

Underline the question in red, the two things to be in blue, the two things not to be in green, and the promise in yellow. Have kids do the same on their Scripture Cards. Challenge kids to tape their Scripture Cards to the bathroom mirror so they see it and repeat the verse each morning and evening.

... Do not be terrified; do not be discouraged, for the Lord your God will be with you wherever you go. Joshua 1:9

WEEK 3—GROWING THE WORD

Before this activity, cut a 2-foot length of 14-gauge wire for each child. You will also need poster board, scissors, masking tape, and markers.

Invite groups of four kids to repeat Joshua 1:9, with each taking one of the 1-2-2-1 portions you learned last week. Remind kids that God is with us always and wherever we go. Then ask:

❥ **How does God's promise of being with us help our faith in him grow?**

❥ **When is it especially comforting to know that God is with us?**

❥ **How can we help others feel more secure and peaceful? closer to God?**

Tell kids they'll make cool Scripture Pets to take with them wherever they go. Show kids how to cut a 3-by-6-inch strip of poster-board "collar." Write Joshua 1:9 on the collar, then use colorful markers to decorate it. Poke one end of the wire through the collar and tape it on the underside to hold the wire in place. The wire will be the "leash." Twist a small loop "handle" in the end of the wire opposite the collar. When you hold the handle, the leash should stay stiffly off the ground as if there's an invisible pet wearing the collar! Walk your pets around the room as you repeat Joshua 1:9.

WEEK 4—SHOWING THE WORD

Write Joshua 1:9 on two large sheets of newsprint or poster board and cut each sheet into ten puzzle pieces. Have a tape dispenser and colored markers ready for the relay below. You'll also need one smooth stone for each person.

Form two lines of kids. Hand tape to the person on one end of each line and the markers to the person on the other end. The kids in between are the relayers who will hold the puzzle pieces. They are to pass puzzle pieces one at a time to the players with tape to reassemble the verse. When the verse is assembled into its correct order, they are to pass it to the person with the marker, who will underline the 1-2-2-1 sentences in the verse. When the verse is reassembled and underlined, teams are to repeat it aloud. Review the 1-2-2-1 pattern and remind kids that God is with us everywhere we go.

Have kids remain in their groups and read aloud Psalm 139:1-10, then discuss the following questions:

❥ **How does it feel to know that God knows our going in and coming out, that is, everything we do and every place we go?**

❥ **How should knowing God is with us all the time affect our choices? how we treat others? the words we say?**

Hand each child a smooth stone and use markers to draw a red heart on each stone. Have kids hold their heart stones as you share a prayer thanking God for his constant presence. Then challenge kids to carry the heart stones with them every day for a week to remind them of God's continual presence in their lives.

WEEK 1—SOWING THE WORD.

Write Joshua 1:8, 9 on two sheets of newsprint, one verse on each sheet. Attach the sheets to a door or wall for learners to read. You'll also need markers, copies of the Scripture Card from page 128 and copies of the Weekly Word Journal from page 84.

Have everyone read Joshua 1:8, 9 two times from the newsprint. Explain that these verses are some of the most powerful and peaceful verses in Scripture because they tell us what to do with God's Word and remind us that God is with us at all times.

Point out that Joshua 1:8, 9 contain commands and promises from God. Invite a volunteer to read verse 8 aloud, then place a green exclamation mark beside the verse and underline in green the part that contains a command from God. Ask for another volunteer to place a red heart beside the portion of the verse that contains a promise from God, then underline the promise in red. Continue in the same way for verse 9, which also contains commands and a promise.

Have learners do the same with their Scripture Cards. Distribute the Weekly Word Journals. Keep the newsprint verses to use next week.

WEEK 2—KNOWING THE WORD

Have learners repeat Joshua 1:8, 9 one time using the verses written on the newsprint and observing the commands and promises you identified last week. Then invite pairs to repeat verses 8 and 9 aloud, with each person repeating one verse.

Explain that the commands and promises in these two verses tell us about the importance of relying on God's Word to be with us all the time just as we know God is always with us. Explain that in Hebrew, the word for meditate means "to repeat continually" or "to speak" (as in Psalm 1:2). Read aloud verse 8 and ask:

- ❧ **How does knowing that meditate doesn't just mean "think about" but also "repeat continually" affect your view of learning God's Word? using God's Word? valuing his Word?**
- ❧ **What clues does verse 8 give us about using God's Word and what it will do for us?**
- ❧ **Why is it important to our faith to know that God and his Word are with us continually, perpetually affecting our lives?**

End with a prayer thanking God for his Word and for the ability to meditate on it in the fullest sense. Close with a corporate "amen," then repeat Joshua 1:8, 9.

WEEK 3—GROWING THE WORD

Enlarge, copy, and cut apart the situations at the end of this activity, so each person will have one. Place each set of five paper strips in an envelope. Cut the newsprint verses into as many pieces as there are learners.

... Do not be discouraged, for the Lord your God will be with you wherever you go. Joshua 1:8, 9

Distribute the pieces and begin by repeating Joshua 1:8, 9 two times. Then see how quickly the verses can be reassembled. Repeat the verse once more. Remind everyone that God and his Word are with us continually and in every situation and place. Have learners form groups of five, then give each group an envelope. Have people discuss the strips in relation to Joshua 1:8, 9 and in terms of these questions:

> ❧ **How does this situation cause worry, fear, discouragement, or anxiety?**
> ❧ **If this situation can't be corrected immediately, how does knowing God is with us help us persevere?**

Have small groups pray for our faith in God's presence through any situation and for the commitment to keep learning his Word as commanded. Encourage learners to put their situation strips in their Bibles as bookmarks to remind them that no situation is too big for God because he is with us in every one of them!

❧ *You just discovered that you have a serious illness.*
❧ *Someone in the family just lost a job.*
❧ *A teacher or supervisor at work doesn't like you.*
❧ *An elderly parent or grandparent is moving in with you.*
❧ *You or your family is moving out of state.*

WEEK 4—SHOWING THE WORD

Hand each participant a slip of paper and a pen. Invite them to list the answers to the following:

❧ *your favorite place to go*
❧ *the first name of your least favorite person*
❧ *your scariest thought or fear*

❧ *your biggest worry today*
❧ *the first name of a loved one*
❧ *your favorite way to worship or praise God*

Remind everyone that God is with us all the time and that he commands us to learn his Word and use it in our lives. Then repeat Joshua 1:8, 9 one time aloud. Explain that you'll use the things listed in a responsive prayer. When you read a sentence, learners can silently read their responses, then everyone will say, "God is with me." For example, if you say, "When I am at . . ." learners are to fill in the blank with the first thing listed, then respond with, "God is with me." Close the prayer with a corporate "amen."

When I am at . . . (first response)
When I am face to face with . . . (second response)
When I am afraid of . . . (third response)
When I'm troubled by . . . (fourth response)
When I enjoy time with . . . (fifth response)
And when I praise you by . . . (sixth response)
Thank you, God, for being with me all the time and for your Word, which gives me comfort continually. Amen.

August

WEEK 1

Read Joshua 1:8, 9, then verse 7. Compare and contrast verse 7 with verse 9 as you answer these questions on another sheet of paper.

❧ Why do you think the same command ("Be strong and courageous") was given in two verses so close together?

❧ What is similar in verses 7 and 8? How does keeping God's Word close help our obedience? faith? courage level?

❧ What plan can you initiate to learn, meditate on, and apply God's Word this week? How might planning a set time of learning Scripture help your relationship with God?

WEEK 3

Read Joshua 1:1-11 and consider *when* God promised Joshua his presence. Joshua was taking over Moses' leadership, and God wanted the ground rules set so Joshua would know he had divine power and strength behind him.

❧ How did God's words prepare Joshua for strenuous military campaigns? How is this like God getting us ready for strenuous campaigns every day as we go out "into the world"?

_____
_____

❧ Joshua obeyed God and succeeded at conquering his enemies. How is this like the success we enjoy when we obey God's command to learn his Word and trust that he is with us?

_____
_____

❧ Outline a battle plan for a situation that is troubling you. Include two ways you can obey God and two ways you can use God's presence and his Word to fight the "enemy."

_____
_____

WEEK 2

Joshua 1:7-9 deals with God's presence and the value of learning God's Word, but the connection between the two is not readily apparent.

❧ In what specific ways are these two themes related?

_____
_____

❧ How does keeping God's Word on our lips affect our actions, attitudes, and words?

_____
_____

❧ How is God's presence in our lives reinforced by his Word in our hearts and minds?

_____
_____

❧ List on the back three areas of your life that could use more of God's presence and his Word. Now look up these areas or key words for these areas in a concordance to see what the Bible has to say about them!

WEEK 4

The English word *meditate* means to think about or contemplate. In Hebrew, the word for meditate (*hagah*) had a slightly different meaning: to speak or repeat constantly. Although we understand meditation as a silent activity, God most likely wanted his people to *actively* meditate on his Word. Choose a word from Joshua 1:7-9 to meditate on in an active sense. For example, you might choose the word *command* and explore what God means by writing out your thoughts, finding the word in the concordance and reading verses that contain it, repeating the word when you ask someone to do something or when someone asks you, or learning a verse containing *command*. Use the following ways to actively meditate on your word: write it, speak it, think it, read it, use it.

August

WEEK 1—Look at the Book!

Read aloud Joshua 1:9 and identity the various portions and phrases in the verse. Have each family member choose one portion to meditate on during the coming week. For example, someone might choose the part that says, "be strong and courageous" or "do not be discouraged." After everyone has chosen a portion of the verse, have family members write their part on a sheet of white paper and decorate it with markers. Photocopy each page and assemble them into books for each family member. Work during the week to concentrate and remember one portion, then choose a new portion next week!

WEEK 3—Phylactery Placemats

Purchase a vinyl placemat for each family member. You'll also need permanent markers, tacky craft glue, and two 4-by-5-inch rectangles of fabric for each person. Glue the fabric to the fronts of the placemats, one on the right and one on the left. Glue three sides of each rectangle to make fabric "pockets" that are open at the top. Decorate the placemats using permanent markers. As the placemats dry, have everyone copy different verses on slips of paper to slide in one of the placemat pockets. Use the words from Joshua 1:8, 9; Psalm 139:1-10; or Deuteronomy 11:18-20. Use the other pocket for napkins or tableware. Read a verse before and after each meal.

WEEK 2—Always-Here Key Chains

Pick up colorful Formica laminate samples at a home center store. These samples have holes drilled in one end to fit on key chains. You'll also need key chains or satin cord, paint pens, glitter glue, and small pictures of your family. Make sure each person has a picture of every family member, then arrange and glue the pictures to the laminate chips. Use markers to write Joshua 1:9b on the backs, then attach key chains or cords. Decorate around the pictures with glitter glue and markers before setting them aside to dry. Challenge family members to carry their key chains all week as a reminder that God and our families are always with us and loving us!

God will be with you wherever you go. Joshua 1:9

WEEK 4—God's Winners!

Read the story of David and Goliath from 1 Samuel 17. Explain that God was with David every moment, which made David strong and courageous. And even though Goliath seemed too big to conquer, God had the victory just as he does with all our fears and troubles! Make a giant Goliath from white shelf paper and tape it to a door. Then write any fears, worries, or troubles family members may have on small slips of paper. Pray as a family for each fear or worry, then tape the slips of paper to Goliath to show that, just as God had victory over Goliath, God has victory over our worries.

Fun Family Activities

BEING TEACHABLE

2 Timothy 3:16, 17

PLANTING THE SEEDS

September is the month that begins most back-to-school celebrations and beginnings. Teaching, learning, and seeing the results of hard work mark school years, but they should characterize all lives for a lifetime! What a perfect time of year to learn how God's Word teaches and guides us in so many powerful ways! Yet even though we know the teaching power of Scripture and the wondrous gift God has given us in his Word, many of us have a hard time settling down to learn exactly what God's Word says and may spend even less time looking for ways to apply it. We might even ask, "*Why* should I learn God's Word?" To that question, 2 Timothy supplies a complete answer in a straightforward, simple way.

PRE K–K (2 Timothy 3:16a). Young children are just being introduced to the Bible and God's Word; in fact, they probably don't even realize that the big word *Scripture* refers to God's Word! In 2 Timothy 3:16 kids will discover why we're to learn God's Word in a simple way—because it's useful!

ELEMENTARY (2 Timothy 3:16). Older kids have a favorite question in school and in church: "*Why* do I need to learn that?" God supplies the perfect answer to that question in 2 Timothy 3:16 and gives a whole class full of doubting Thomases specific, real-life reasons for the importance of God's Word and how it serves us.

YOUTH/ADULT (2 Timothy 3:16, 17). Older teens and adults are often glad to be in an arena where Scripture memory and discovery aren't stressed as greatly as in kids' classes or at school. Is it because they believe they can't memorize? Could it be they are "too busy"? Whatever the reason, 2 Timothy 3:16, 17 is a powerful reminder of all that God's Word is and does for us. Plus, 2 Timothy 3:16, 17 tells all those who want to do good that God's Word equips us for *every* good work!

SECRET SCRIPTURE SIGNAL

Each month a new Scripture signal is suggested as a fun way of signaling someone in your church or family to repeat the month's key verse! For this month's Scripture signal, say the word *tractor* to remind others of the t-r-c-t-r pattern of verse 16. Each time you or a friend says the word *tractor,* repeat the verses, then see if you can tell what each letter in t-r-c-t-r stands for.

GARDENING TIPS

❦ Kids might enjoy using their own breaths to make pretty Scripture pictures as they remember that all Scripture is God-breathed. Put drops of food coloring on a paper and use drinking straws to gently blow the drops. Write 2 Timothy 3:16 on the pictures.

❦ Challenge youth and adults to write a "tractor" allegory about Scripture to show how both work to plant seeds that grow good fruit.

❦ Start a whole-church or family brainstorm list of all the things Scripture is useful for. Begin the list with the five items mentioned in 2 Timothy 3:16, 17, then place markers beside the list and let people add to it over the next few weeks.

God's Word is useful for . . .

Psalm 119:11 _____   Acts 17:11 _____

_____   _____

_____   _____

Psalm 119:98 _____   Proverbs 3:5, 6 _____

_____   _____

_____   _____

Psalm 119:105 _____   Matthew 6:14 _____

_____   _____

_____   _____

WEEK 1—SOWING THE WORD

Before class, make one copy of the Fun Family Activities from page 95 for each child.

Have children breathe on their hands as you point out that each breath they take gives them ongoing life. Then explain that you'll be learning a verse about God's breath today and how it gives life to his Word. Repeat 2 Timothy 3:16a two times aloud and invite children to repeat it with you echo-style. Tell children that the Bible contains God's Word, which we call *Scripture.* Point out that Scripture is made to be learned and used in our lives for everything we do and say.

Teach children the following action rhyme based on 2 Timothy 3:16a. Lead children in the accompanying actions and repeat the rhyme three times until children are familiar with the words and the actions.

All Scripture is God-breathed and useful for
What we do and what we say, (Shake your finger, then point to your mouth.)
When we work and when we play. (Pretend to shovel, then hop up and down.)
Let's thank God for his Word each day, (Point upward.)
And use his Word in every way! (Clap your hands three times.)

Close by repeating 2 Timothy 3:16a one time, then pass out the Fun Family Activities.

WEEK 2—KNOWING THE WORD

You'll need balloons, curling ribbon, and the Scripture Card from page 126.

Lead children in the action rhyme you learned last week. Repeat the rhyme several times, then have children repeat 2 Timothy 3:16a with you twice. Remind children that God gave us the Bible and that all Scripture comes from God.

Have children blow a breath out and remind them that God breathes life and truth into his Word. Explain that, just as we breathe so we can live and do good things, the Bible is God-breathed so it does the good things God wants it to do.

Distribute the balloons and have children blow them up, then help tie knots in the balloons. (If you have very young children, you may wish to blow up and tie off the balloons before class.) Tell children that, just as they breathed air into the balloons to make them useful for play, God breathes truth into his Word to make it useful in our lives.

Let children gently bop their balloons up and down as they repeat the action rhyme and 2 Timothy 3:16a several times. Attach a bit of curling ribbon and let children tape the Scripture Cards to the ribbon, then allow children to take the balloons home. Encourage children to have their families help them learn the words to the verse this week.

All Scripture is God-breathed and is useful. 2 Timothy 3:16

WEEK 3—GROWING THE WORD

You'll need crackers, plastic knives, peanut butter, and jelly. You'll also want damp paper towels for quick cleanup.

Lead children in the action rhyme and in repeating 2 Timothy 3:16a several times. Then ask children the following questions:

❧ **Who gave us the Bible?** (God)
❧ **What is Scripture?** (God's Word)
❧ **Who breathed life and truth into Scripture?** (God)

Explain that God's Word is useful for many things. It teaches us truth, tells us about Jesus' love and forgiveness, and teaches us what's right and wrong in God's eyes. Tell children that all Scripture is God-breathed and useful for teaching many things, which we can teach to others. Then have children form pairs or trios and "teach" each other to make peanut butter and jelly cracker sandwiches.

After everyone has a sandwich, nibble them as you chat about all that God's Word teaches us. End by repeating 2 Timothy 3:16a two times.

WEEK 4—SHOWING THE WORD

Before this activity, purchase small chalkboards from a craft store. If you want, you can also make chalkboards by painting chalkboard paint on smooth pieces of plywood. You'll also need chalk, small pieces of sponge to use as erasers, markers and crayons, glue, and copies of the Scripture Card from page 126.

Begin by having children repeat 2 Timothy 3:16a with you several times. Then ask children what God's Word does for us. Remind them that God's Word is God-breathed and useful for teaching many things, including the truth and what's right and wrong in God's eyes. Tell children that they'll make a fun slate to help teach others, just as God's Word teaches us.

Distribute the chalkboards and invite children to use markers and crayons to decorate the edges. Glue the Scripture Cards to the backs of the chalkboards. Let children practice teaching each other the ABCs, using chalk and the sponges as erasers. (Dampen sponges to really clean the boards!) Then have children draw hearts on the chalkboards and tell them that God gave us his Word because he loves us and wants us to learn and use his Word.

End with a prayer thanking God for his useful Word, then close by repeating 2 Timothy 3:16a. Challenge children to teach someone 2 Timothy 3:16a this week.

WEEK 1—SOWING THE WORD

Before this activity, write 2 Timothy 3:16 on a sheet of newsprint and attach it to a wall or door for kids to read. You'll also need markers and, for each person, one copy each of the Scripture Card from page 127 and the Fun Family Activities from page 95.

Invite kids to read the verse two times aloud with you, then one time silently. Explain that this verse answers the question, "Why should I learn Scripture?" Point out that 2 Timothy 3:16 tells us that God's Word comes directly from God (God-breathed) and is useful for all parts of our lives.

Encourage kids to look for any tricks, patterns, or word games to help them remember the order of the things God's Word is useful for. After kids give their ideas, point out one super way to remember this verse. Have kids take the first letters of the listed words: t-r-c-t-r. Point out how the acronym sounds like the word *tractor* and is easy to remember, because tractors plow the ground so good fruits can grow, just as Scripture makes good fruit in our lives!

Circle the t-r-c-t-r words on the newsprint and have kids do the same on their Scripture Cards. Encourage kids to work on learning the verse this week by remembering the word *tractor*. Distribute the Fun Family Activities. Save the newsprint verse to use during the next few weeks.

WEEK 2—KNOWING THE WORD

Collect white paper, tempera paint, newspapers, tape, fine-tipped markers or pens, and copies of the Scripture Card (page 127). Cover a table with newspaper and set out the craft items. You'll also want damp paper towels for quick cleanup.

Have kids repeat 2 Timothy 3:16 two times by looking at the newsprint verse and picturing the word patterns in their minds. Then challenge kids to repeat the verse without looking. Point out that God's Word is God-breathed, which means God breathed truth and life into his Word so it would be useful in our lives. Using the *tractor* trick from last week, ask kids to repeat what God's Word is useful for and to explain how it produces "good fruit" in our lives.

Then let kids use their fingertips and paint to make plowed "garden rows" on the white paper. After the rows have been plowed, show learners how to make thumbprint "fruits" and "vegetables" in the garden rows. When the pictures are dry, have kids list things Scripture does for us on or above each vegetable, such as teaching, rebuking, or loving. Tape the Scripture Cards to the pictures. Challenge kids to use their pictures as a reminder to ask God every day to use his Word to grow good things in their lives.

All Scripture is God-breathed and is useful for teaching, rebuking, correcting and training.... 2 Timothy 3:16

WEEK 3—GROWING THE WORD

Make one copy of the How-To Manual from page 87 for each person. You'll also need pencils or pens and markers.

Invite pairs of kids to repeat 2 Timothy 3:16. After each repetition, have the entire class say, "Scripture is to be learned and used! Thanks, God!" Remind kids that God's Word is alive and useful for every area of our lives, since it teaches us how to do the things God desires us to do. Point out that Scripture is like God's "how-to manual" for our lives—and his "how-not-to manual," as well!

Let kids stay in pairs or trios and distribute the copies of the How-To Manuals. Have kids work together looking up the references and jotting down what God's Word is useful for or what it teaches us to do or not to do. When kids finish filling out the verses, have them fold over the manuals and decorate the fronts as book covers. Finally, have kids write 2 Timothy 3:16 on the backs of the manuals.

Challenge kids to read their How-To Manuals every day for a week as they learn all that Scripture is useful for and why they need to learn and use God's Word!

WEEK 4—SHOWING THE WORD

Cut the newsprint verse into as many pieces as there are kids. (If your group is large, have kids work in pairs.) Hand each person a piece to the Scripture puzzle, then have kids work together in silence to reassemble 2 Timothy 3:16. When the verse is complete, have kids repeat the verse two times, then give each other high fives.

Review the *tractor* trick and corresponding words in the verse, then remind kids that Scripture is true and meant to be used in our lives every day. Tell kids that they've been learning some of the things that Scripture is useful for but that it's also useful for worshiping and praising God. Read aloud Psalm 119:9-16. After each verse, have kids respond with, "Thank you for your Word, Lord." End with a corporate "amen" and challenge kids to choose one verse from Psalm 119:9-16 to learn over the next several days.

WEEK 1—SOWING THE WORD

Before this activity, write 2 Timothy 3:16, 17 on two sheets of newsprint and attach them to the wall or a door for everyone to see. You'll also need copies of the Weekly Word Journal from page 94, the Scripture Card from page 128, and markers or pens.

Have learners read the verses silently one time, then repeat the verse aloud two times. Explain that these verses tell what God's Word is and why it's useful to learn. Point out that verse 16 is the *what* and that verse 17 is the *why*. Then tell learners there's an easy trick to remember the order of the listed words in verse 16. Write the first letters of the listed words (t-r-c-t-r) on the newsprint and show learners that the acronym phonetically spells out the word *tractor* and that, just as a tractor is used to prepare the ground to grow good fruits, Scripture gives us seeds that grow good fruit. Have learners write t-r-c-t-r on their Scripture Cards.

Challenge learners to use the *tractor* trick to work on learning the verse this week. Give everyone a copy of the Weekly Word Journal and remind people to complete the first activity. Keep the newsprint with the verses on the wall for next week.

WEEK 2—KNOWING THE WORD

Have participants repeat 2 Timothy 3:16, 17 two times aloud, then review the t-r-c-t-r acronym by asking people to name the words in the verse that tell us what God's Word is useful for. Remind everyone that God's Word is to be learned and used in every area of our lives. Then ask:

- **What do you think is meant by the term "God-breathed"? How is this similar to or different from the ideas of "inspired" or "based on"?**
- **In what ways is Scripture truly useful for teaching? rebuking? correcting? training in righteousness?**
- **How does Scripture have the power to change lives? attitudes? affect our relationships with others? with God?**

End by sharing a prayer thanking God for his Word and asking for his help in learning, remembering, and applying Scripture. Close by repeating 2 Timothy 3:16, 17 one time.

WEEK 3—GROWING THE WORD

Photocopy the verse cards from this activity, one verse card for every three people. You'll also need markers or pens.

Invite pairs of learners to repeat 2 Timothy 3:16, 17. Then ask a volunteer to tell what the letters t-r-c-t-r stand for in verse 16.

All Scripture is God-breathed and is useful ... so that the man of God may be thoroughly equipped.... 2 Timothy 3:16, 17

Form trios and hand each group a pen and a verse card. Explain that groups are to look up Scripture verses and give examples of situations that are helped through that particular portion of God's Word. Write the situations on the blanks and try to name at least two for each verse.

When groups are finished writing, have them share their ideas with the entire class. Tabulate how many situations are helped by God's Word. End by having a trio pray for the group and asking for God's conviction in turning to Scripture to help in situations we face every day.

GOD'S WORD HELPS AND HEALS!

Psalm 119:11 _____

Psalm 119:105 _____

Acts 17:11 _____

Proverbs 3:5, 6 _____

Matthew 6:14 _____

WEEK 4—SHOWING THE WORD

Cut the newsprint pieces into as many pieces as there are learners. Then see how quickly the group can reassemble 2 Timothy 3:16, 17. When both verses are put back together, repeat them two times aloud. Remind participants that Scripture equips us to do good works and accomplish great things for God. Point out that you have explored how Scripture helps teach, rebuke, correct, and train us for righteousness in many life situations. Then explain that Scripture also helps us pray.

Have learners read 2 Timothy 3:16, 17 and Psalm 119:9-16 with partners, then work together to compose a prayer using words from these verses. These prayers should ask God for help learning and using Scripture and also praise God for his wisdom, his Word, and his love. Close by having each group read its prayer aloud to God. End with a corporate "amen."

September

WEEK 1

Read 2 Timothy 3:16, 17, then match the goals this verse gives us for God's Word. For example, God's Word is useful for teaching, so the goal would be *learning*.

teaching	good works
rebuking	drawing near God
correcting	repentance
equipping	learning
training in righteousness	direction

➤ If you want to reach these goals, why is it vital to learn, recall, and apply God's Word?

➤ Circle one of the above goals, then study Scripture that will help you meet that goal this week. Use your concordance to look up the word and read what the Bible says about it.

WEEK 3

In the first column below are places where Jesus used Scripture to teach, to rebuke, to correct, or to train in righteousness. The second column lists the Old Testament passage Jesus quoted and the third column the way Scripture helped, as listed in 2 Timothy 3:16. Match the columns to discover what verses Jesus quoted and why. The first one has been done for you.

Matt. 4:4	Isa. 54:13	teaching
Mark 15.34	Deut. 8:3	correcting
John 6:45	Psalm 22:1	rebuking
Matt. 4:7	Deut. 6:13	rebuking
Mark 12:29-30	Deut. 6:16	training in righteousness
Matt. 4:10	Deut. 6:4, 5	rebuking

WEEK 2

We're told in 2 Timothy 3:16, 17 that Scripture is useful for many things and is a part of *every* good work for the person of God. Read Matthew 4:1-11 and Mark 15:34 to learn how Jesus used Scripture, then answer the following questions.

➤ How do we know that Jesus learned, remembered, and applied Scripture?

_____

_____

➤ Why do you think the Son of God learned God's Word? How did he use God's Word?

_____

_____

➤ What does this teach us about the importance of relying on Scripture for every part of *our* lives?

_____

_____

WEEK 4

Second Timothy 3:16, 17 contains three powerful, all-encompassing words that give us clues regarding the great importance of learning and using Scripture: *all, thoroughly,* and *every*. Write these three words and the words that immediately follow.

_____

_____

_____

Now read the words together: "*all* Scripture; *thoroughly* equipped; *every* good work." Powerful, isn't it? In a nutshell, these words give us the all-inclusive power of Scripture! Now, in a nutshell, use the back of this page to write a short paragraph defining the role God's Word plays or should play in your words, actions, and how you relate to God and others.

September

WEEK 1—Mirror, Mirror

Before this neat trick, put a bit of bath soap on your finger and lightly trace the word "Scripture" on a large mirror or window. Let the soap dry so it's invisible, then invite the family to gather around the mirror. Point out that 2 Timothy 3:16 tells us that all Scripture is God-breathed. Remind everyone that God's Word helps us see things more clearly and guides us in every way. Then invite everyone to breathe on the glass so your hidden message appears! Point out that we may not see God's breath on his Word but we see what his Word does in our lives!

WEEK 2—Oh So Wise

Have family members each choose a verse or two from Proverbs to write on index cards, then read aloud. Take turns identifying how God's Word in these verses helps us and when you could put that wisdom to work in your life. Remind everyone that God's Word makes us wise, guides us away from bad things, and leads us toward goodness and grace! Collect the index cards into a booklet and photocopy the cards so each family member has a copy to read and refer to often for God's wisdom and truth.

WEEK 3—On the Right Track-tor!

Remember t-r-c-t-r or the *tractor* trick in 2 Timothy 3:16? Enlarge the simple tractor illustration on a large sheet of poster board and have the family work to decorate the tractor and write the words that t-r-c-t-r stands for. Then color and cut out the tractor and embellish it by gluing on nuts, bolts, screws, and washers. Hang the tractor in a place where your family can view it often. As you discover more things God's Word does for us, list them on your special tractor and share them with family members.

WEEK 4—Gift Lift!

One of the greatest gifts God has given us is his Word! Share God's Word with family and friends by photocopying Bible verses or writing Scripture on colorful paper. Choose cheerful, uplifting verses such as Galatians 5:13, Ephesians 4:32, or Philippians 4:13. Roll the papers into scrolls and tie them with ribbons. Have each family member make three rolls. Then spend an afternoon together distributing your gifts of love to neighbors, friends, local shopkeepers, and others who could use a wonderful gift—and lift! (God's Word is useful for bringing love and smiles, too!)

Fun Family Activities

HARVESTTIME

Galatians 5:22, 23, 25

PLANTING THE SEEDS

Wheat is sheaved, corn plucked from the fields, apples snatched from treetops, and pumpkins rolled into piles awaiting turns at becoming spicy pies. So go the harvest days of October, filled with good food, good fun—and good fruit! It's the ideal time of year to focus on the good fruit that we bear through the help of the Holy Spirit—God's foremost harvest helper! Galatians 5:22, 23, 25 fill a cornucopia of our best to God and others through living by and keeping step with the Holy Spirit as we seek to grow, harvest, and share the spiritual fruit that feeds us all!

PRE K–K (Galatians 5:22a). Young children adore harvesttime with its bright colors of plump pumpkins, spicy apples and cider, and all the other wonderful foods autumn brings! Galatians 5:22 is a fun verse to learn as children discover that, just as gardens grow good things to eat and make us happy and thankful, we can grow good things in our lives to make us happy and thankful. Young children will be learning the first portion of Galatians 5:22 but will be exposed to all the spiritual fruit names in a colorful finger rhyme.

ELEMENTARY (Galatians 5:22, 23). Older kids enjoy the breath of cool, crisp air that flies in on the wings of October. Harvesttime holds the promise of football, falling leaves, and rising appetites for all the good foods of fall! Galatians 5:22, 23 reminds kids that we're fed upon God's Word and goodness and that, as we grow good things in our lives, we can feed others and share with them God's bountiful love!

YOUTH/ADULT (Galatians 5:22, 23, 25). Even older teens and adults can't help but feel the excitement at the change of seasons and the coziness ushered in with October, from leaves and sheaves to frost and good foods. Galatians 5:22, 23, 25 remind youth and adults that they can bear their own good fruit, which doesn't last for just one growing season but for an entire lifetime. Help adults and teens remember that nothing grows or flourishes without care, constancy, and the help of the Spirit!

SECRET SCRIPTURE SIGNAL

Each month a new Scripture signal is suggested as a fun way of signaling someone in your church or family to repeat the month's key verse! For October's Scripture signal, make cupped hands, such as holding apples or as a cornucopia. Each time you give the Secret Scripture Signal or someone signals you, repeat the verse and give the other person a high five!

GARDENING TIPS

- Make a harvest display to remind everyone of the spiritual fruit listed in Galatians 5:22, 23. Place sheaves against a wall and let children write the word for each spiritual fruit on a pumpkin or gourd and set them beside the sheaves. Write out Galatians 5:22, 23 on a length of poster board and use wire to attach it to the sheaves.
- As a church service project, have kids use permanent markers and write the fruit of the Spirit on real fruits to hand to everyone in church. Write one word on each fruit, using oranges, bananas, pears, and various colors of apples.

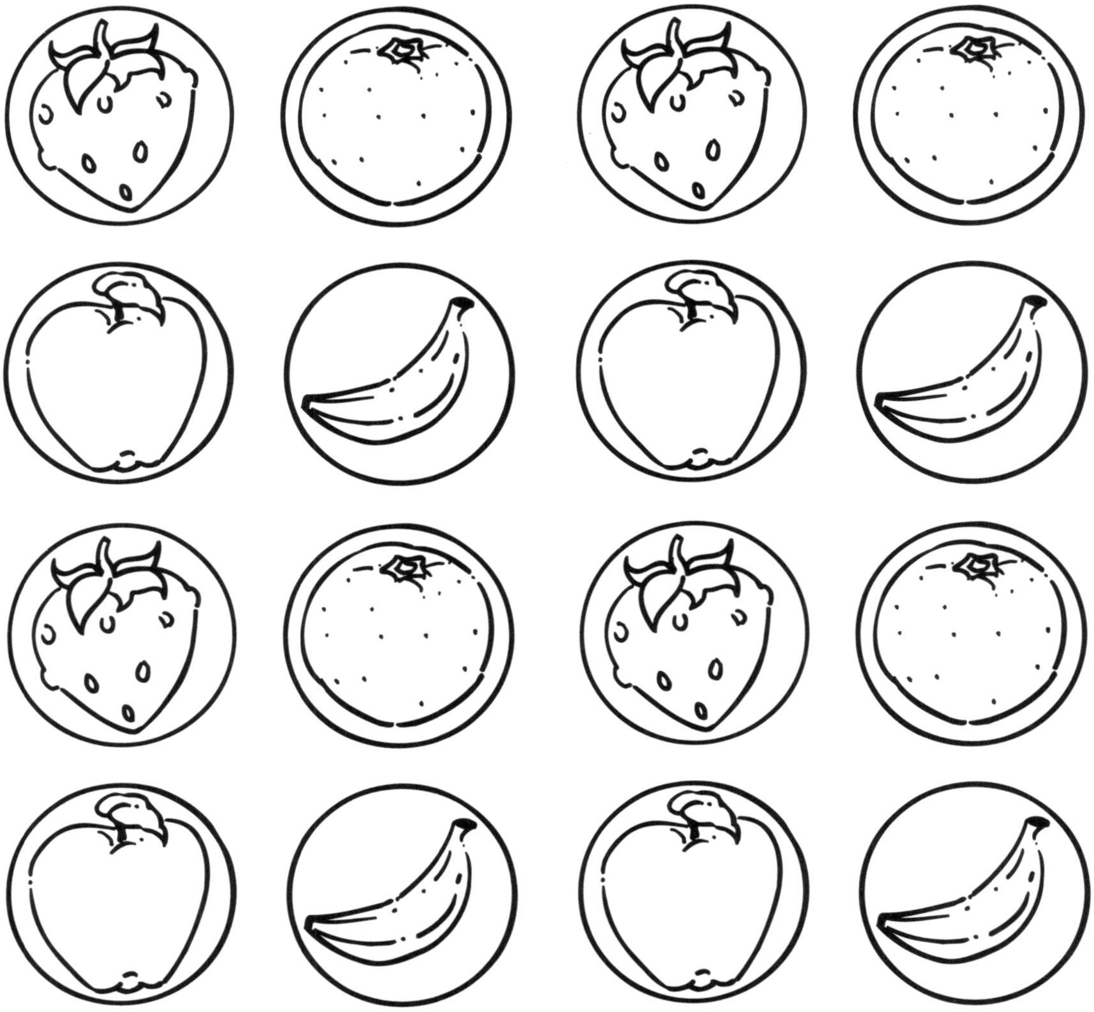

WEEK 1—SOWING THE WORD

Copy on stiff paper the Fruit of the Spirit icons from page 97. Cut out and tape the icons to plastic spoon handles. You'll need a set of icons for each child plus one for yourself. Copy the Fruit Salad rhyme below and the Fun Family Activities from page 105.

Place the spoons beside you and tell the children they'll begin to learn a verse about growing good things and how the Holy Spirit helps us do that. Repeat the rhyme using the spoons. Lead children in using their own icon spoons as you repeat the rhyme two more times.

Repeat Galatians 5:22a, "But the fruit of the Spirit is love, joy, peace," then ask children to repeat the verse with you echo-style two times. Help children tape the Fruit Salad rhyme to their icon spoons and encourage them to ask their families to help them learn the rhyme this week. Hand out the Fun Family Activities.

FRUIT SALAD

Fruit salad, fruit salad, good in the tummy—
Here's the good fruit that makes it so yummy! Take ...
Peace, love, and kindness; (apple spoon)
Self-control and goodness; (orange spoon)
Patience, joy, and gentleness— (banana spoon)
Add a heart of faithfulness. (strawberry spoon)
Toss it all together; let your love be in it, (Hold all spoons.)
And you'll enjoy deliciously
God's fruit of the Spirit! (Wave spoons in the air.)

WEEK 2—KNOWING THE WORD

You'll need an apple for every two children, tempera paints, newspapers, tape, plastic spoons, white paper, and photocopies of the Scripture Card from page 126. Cover a table with newspapers and set out the tempera paints and white paper.

Repeat the Fruit Salad rhyme you learned last week, then lead children in repeating Galatians 5:22a two times aloud. Remind children that the Holy Spirit helps us grow good things in our lives, such as love, joy, and peace. Point out that trees grow good fruit to eat and to give us energy to do good things. In the same way, God's Spirit helps us grow good fruit in our lives to do good things.

Give each child an apple quarter and show kids how to use a plastic spoon to carve an interesting design on the apple. Then let children use their carved apples to make apple prints on the paper. Tape the Scripture Cards for Galatians 5:22a across the tops of the pictures. Close by having children repeat Galatians 5:22a two times aloud, then hand out the rest of the apples to nibble and crunch.

WEEK 3—GROWING THE WORD

Before this activity, cut out construction-paper fruit, including apples, oranges, and bananas. Cut out one piece of fruit for each child plus a set of fruit to use in a game. Write the word *love* on the apples, *peace* on the oranges, and *joy* on the bananas. Tape one set of fruit to the floor but scatter them so they're about six feet apart.

Repeat the Fruit Salad rhyme, then repeat Galatians 5:22a twice. Ask children:
➤ **Who helps us grow good things in our lives?** (the Holy Spirit, God)
➤ **How does love help us? joy? peace?**

Distribute the paper fruit and tell children the apples are for love, the oranges for peace, and the bananas for joy. Play a game calling out fruit of the Spirit and having children holding those fruits hop to the matching fruit on the floor. For example, when you say "joy," have children with bananas hop to the joy banana and say, "The fruit of the Spirit is joy!" When you say, "Fruit salad!" have children choose a different fruit to hop to. End by thanking the Spirit for love, peace, and joy.

WEEK 4—SHOWING THE WORD

Bring in a real fruit for each child, including apples, bananas, oranges, pears, and peaches. You'll also need miniature marshmallows, plastic knives, peanut butter, and tiny candies.

Form three groups and have one be the love group, one be the peace group, and one be the joy group. Repeat Galatians 5:22a and, when you get to "love, joy, peace," have each group shout its special word. Have children in the groups give each other high fives, then remind them that love, joy, and peace are good things to have in our lives and share with others. Explain you'll make good fruit to share with others and remind them that the Holy Spirit helps us grow good things in our lives.

Let each child choose a piece of fruit to decorate. Using peanut butter "glue," attach marshmallows and candies to make fruity faces, hair, and other features. As children work, remind them that sharing with others is a way to show our love and joy.

When the fruit people are finished, challenge children to share their good fruit with family members or friends and to tell them about the good things God wants us to have in our lives. (Other classes are bringing fruits home to share as well!)

WEEK 1—SOWING THE WORD

Write Galatians 5:22, 23 on newsprint and tape it where kids can see it. You'll need markers and copies of the Scripture Card from page 127 and the Fun Family Activities from page 105.

Have children read aloud the verses two times, then explain that these verses teach us what the Holy Spirit helps us grow in our lives, which brings us closer to God and to others. Point out that there are nine characteristics the Spirit helps us have in our lives and show how you can group them in three groups of three by the number of syllables in each word. The words *love, joy,* and *peace* each have one syllable (underline these words in red). The words *patience, kindness,* and *goodness* each have two syllables (underline in blue). And the words *faithfulness, gentleness,* and *self-control* each have three syllables (underline in yellow). There's a 1-2-3 pattern!

Have learners use markers to underline the words on their Scripture Cards and write a red 1, a blue 2, and a yellow 3 on their cards. Challenge kids to use the 1-2-3 syllable pattern to learn the verse this week. Hand out the Fun Family Activities.

WEEK 2—KNOWING THE WORD

Create a construction-paper tree on the wall in a hallway or other place where people will be able to enjoy the display. You'll also need real apples to eat (one for every four kids), tape, scissors, markers, construction paper, and plastic knives.

Lead kids in repeating Galatians 5:22, 23 two times, then ask kids to identify the fruit of the Spirit using the 1-2-3 pattern of syllables you learned last week. Remind kids that the Spirit helps us grow good things in our lives to share with others and bring us nearer to God. Hand each child a quarter of an apple to eat, then ask:

❧ **How is the Spirit's work in our lives like an apple nourishing us?**
❧ **How can the fruit of the Spirit help us every day? draw us closer to God?**
❧ **What do you think it means that, "Against such things there is no law"?**

Have kids write the fruit of the Spirit on pieces of paper fruit, one per paper fruit, then tape them to the tree in the hall as a reminder to others that the Spirit will help us grow good things in our lives. End with a prayer thanking the Spirit for giving us good fruit to put to work in our lives and to draw us closer to God.

WEEK 3—GROWING THE WORD

Copy the recipe on page 101 for each child. You'll also need softened cream cheese, brown sugar, plastic bowls and spoons, and apple slices.

Invite pairs of kids to repeat Galatians 5:22, 23 aloud, then choose the next pair to repeat the verse. Give each other high fives after each successful repetition. Have kids name the fruit of the Spirit according to the 1-2-3 syllable pattern, then

But the fruit of the Spirit is love, joy, peace, patience, kindness, goodness, faithfulness, gentleness, self-control.... Galatians 5:22, 23

ask them why God would want us to use this fruit once it is grown in our lives. Explain that learning what to do with the fruit of the Spirit is much like a recipe helping us know what to do with ingredients. Invite kids to use the recipes to prepare the caramel apple dip.

As kids enjoy their apple slices and dip in small groups, discuss how we can use each of the nine traits in Galatians 5:22, 23 in our lives. End by encouraging the kids to take home their recipes and to make this sweet treat for their families and friends as they remind them of the good fruit God's Spirit produces in our lives.

Caramel Apple Dip

You'll need:
- ❥ a bowl and spoon
- ❥ a large package of cream cheese
- ❥ 1 cup of brown sugar

Combine a large package of softened cream cheese and a cup of brown sugar in a bowl. Cream the brown sugar and cream cheese together until the mixture is smooth. Dip apple slices or other pieces of fruit in this yummy dip for a happy harvest treat! (Makes enough for five to seven delighted dippers!)

WEEK 4—SHOWING THE WORD

You'll need one orange for each child plus one extra. Use a red permanent marker to draw a heart on each orange.

Repeat Galatians 5:22, 23 and when you get to the list of nine traits, have nine different kids each name one fruit of the Spirit. Continue repeating the verse until each child has a turn to name a fruit. Use the 1-2-3 pattern to review the entire list, then remind everyone that just *having* these fruits isn't enough—God wants us to put them to use in our lives!

Sit in a circle on the floor and have everyone silently think of a spiritual fruit from the list of nine to work on growing and using for the next two weeks. Then share a prayer asking the Holy Spirit to guide you in not only growing good fruit in your lives but in sharing it with God and others. Pray: **Dear Lord, we ask for your help and the help of the Holy Spirit to guide us growing good things in our lives. We know the fruit we grow can be shared with others and will draw us closer to you. Please help us grow ...** (roll the orange back and forth around the circle as each child names the spiritual fruit he has chosen to grow and use). **In Jesus' name we pray, amen.**

Close by handing each child an orange to share at home. (Other classes are receiving fruit to share, so families can create a fruit salad to share at home.)

WEEK 1—SOWING THE WORD

Write the words to Galatians 5:22, 23, 25 on three sheets of newsprint and attach them to the wall. You'll also need markers and one photocopy of the Scripture Card for Galatians 5:22, 23, 25 from page 128 and the Weekly Word Journal from page 104 for each person.

Hand out the Scripture Cards and markers. Invite learners to repeat the two verses two times aloud. Point out that verses 22 and 23 contain a list of things the Holy Spirit helps us grow in our lives. Then circle the first three spiritual words in the list and point out how each has one syllable. Then circle the next three words and explain that they each have two syllables. Finally, circle the last three words and note that they each contain three syllables. Have learners do the same on their cards and write the numerals 1, 2, and 3 in the margin. Point out how four of the words end in the suffix -*ness*.

Invite volunteers to name all nine traits the Spirit produces according to their syllables. Explain that the order of the fruits doesn't matter nearly as much as recalling each one in some order! (At least with the syllables, they'll be close!)

Encourage participants to tape their Scripture Cards on their refrigerators to practice each time they open the door for "good fruits" or other good things to eat. Remind them that God's Word feeds us when we take the time to learn and use it! Hand out the Weekly Word Journals. Keep the newsprint pages on the wall for next week.

WEEK 2—KNOWING THE WORD

Before this activity, you'll need to gather paper, pens or pencils, a knife, and an apple for every two people.

Have everyone repeat Galatians 5:22, 23, 25 aloud two times, then see if learners can recite the entire list of the fruit of the Spirit. Remind people that the Holy Spirit helps us grow these qualities in our lives so we can feed ourselves and others on God's love.

Cut the apples in half and hand each person a half but tell learners not to eat their apples yet. Form small groups and have people discuss these questions:
- **How many apples do you think one apple tree could bear? How many more apple trees and apples might grow from the seeds inside each apple on a tree?**
- **What does this tell us about the good fruit we grow in our own lives? How can that good fruit grow and produce more good fruit in others?**
- **How does living by and keeping in step with the Holy Spirit help us grow this spiritual fruit? use the fruit?**

Have small groups share the highlights of their answers with everyone. Then repeat Galatians 5:22, 23, 25 aloud two times. End with a prayer thanking the Holy Spirit for helping us grow God's fruit in our lives, then munch your apple halves.

The fruit of the Spirit is love, joy, peace.... Since we live by the Spirit, let us keep in step with the Spirit. Galatians 5:22, 23, 25

WEEK 3—GROWING THE WORD

You'll need small to medium-sized clay pots, potting soil, flower or vegetable seeds, a spritzer bottle of water, spoons, and colored permanent markers. Cover a table with newspapers, then set out the potting soil, seeds, spoons, and water.

Have everyone write Galatians 5:22, 23 on a pot. Have learners fill their pots three-quarters full with potting soil. As people work to fill the pots, ask:

> ❧ **How can we prepare ourselves to plant seeds of love, joy, peace, patience, kindness, goodness, faithfulness, gentleness, and self-control in our lives?**

Then have people each plant nine seeds in their pots. As they do so, ask:

> ❧ **What are the nine seeds the Holy Spirit helps us grow in our lives? How can living by the Spirit help our spiritual fruit grow?**
> ❧ **In what ways can growing each seed in our lives help draw us closer to God and others?**

Finally, have learners cover the seeds with soil, then gently spritz the "gardens" with water. Ask:

> ❧ **How can we tend the good fruit in our lives so it will bear generously?**
> ❧ **In what specific ways can we pass the fruit of our harvest on to others?**

Tell participants to silently think of one spiritual fruit they'd like to work on growing over the next few weeks. Then offer a prayer asking the Spirit's help in nurturing the seeds you've planted in your hearts to help them grow into good fruit that touches others. Tell people to watch the growth of their own good fruit as the plants in their gardens are tended and grow!

WEEK 4—SHOWING THE WORD

Practice this neat trick before class so you can demonstrate how to prepare the bananas for everyone to take home. You'll need toothpicks and a banana for each person plus one extra for you to use in this devotional activity. (Choose bananas that have tiny brown spots and aren't overly ripe.) Prepare one banana by poking a toothpick at 1-inch intervals down the side of the banana. Each time you poke the toothpick in the banana, move it back and forth to slice the banana inside the peeling. When you unpeel the banana, it will be already sliced and amaze your audience!

Repeat Galatians 5:22, 23, 25 aloud two times. Remind everyone that the Holy Spirit helps us grow these fruits to deepen our walk with God and to spread his love to others. Hold up the secretly sliced banana and explain that when we live by the Spirit, he helps us grow special fruit in our lives. It's special because it grows inside us so that when it's revealed (unpeel the banana and hand out the slices) it can be shared with others to grow more good fruit!

Show learners how to do this trick and help them prepare their own bananas. Encourage everyone to share this mini-devotion with family or friends as they explain about the good fruit God wants us to have in our lives.

October

WEEK 1

The English word *fruit* can be used as a singular or plural noun. In Greek, however, one would normally use a plural to talk about nine things such as the ones listed in Galatians 5:22, 23.

❧ Why do you think Paul used the singular word for *fruit* (*karpos*) instead of a plural in this verse? Why did he use *fruit* instead of *values* or *attitudes?*

_____

_____

❧ Is it possible to have just one spiritual fruit in our lives? That is, can you have love and not gentleness or patience without faithfulness?

_____

_____

❧ Why is it important to nurture each spiritual fruit in our lives? How does each balance and complement the other?

_____

_____

WEEK 3

Read Galatians 5:25, then answer these questions on a separate sheet of paper.

❧ What does it mean to live by the Spirit? to keep in step with the Spirit?

❧ How are living by and keeping step with the Holy Spirit connected? Can you do one without the other? Explain.

❧ What things keep you from keeping in step with the Spirit? How can you stay in harmony with how the Spirit lives and moves?

❧ In what ways does living in and keeping step with the Holy Spirit help us grow the fruit of the Spirit that Galatians 5:22, 23 talk about?

WEEK 2

Read Galatians 5:22, 23. Paul listed nine wonderful qualities we're to have in our lives, but is this list complete? List other fruit of the Spirit, such as forgiveness or mercy, and give biblical references to support your choices. The first one has been done for you.

forgiveness   Ephesians 4:32

_____

_____

_____

_____

_____

_____

WEEK 4

Read Galatians 5:22, 23, 25. Now let's take a peek in the mirror and see how well you're nurturing and using this special spiritual fruit! On a scale of one to five (with five being highest), how would you rate yourself on growing and using each fruit?

LOVE	JOY
PEACE	PATIENCE
KINDNESS	GOODNESS
FAITHFULNESS	GENTLENESS
SELF-CONTROL	

❧ What can you do to strengthen any fruit that rated a three or below?

_____

_____

October

WEEK 1—Fruit Frappés

Let family members share in the fun of making this delicious and refreshing treat! Purchase clear plastic parfait glasses at a discount house, then layer fresh fruits such as strawberries, blueberries, and peaches with vanilla yogurt. Top off your colorful goodies with a dollop of yogurt and a sprinkling of crunchy granola. As you enjoy your treats, discuss the nine qualities mentioned in Galatians 5:22, 23 and why each is important to have in our lives.

WEEK 3—Harvest Game

Enlarge the game board illustration on stiff paper and use markers or crayons to color the spaces and the fruit. Place colored, fruit-flavored cereal loops on the pictures of the gameboard fruit. You'll move penny markers around the board to collect each different fruit. You can roll a dice cube to determine the number of moves or write the numbers from 1 to 6 on slips of paper, then turn the slips face down and choose one. When someone collects all nine pieces of fruit, she must name the fruit of the Spirit from Galatians 5:22, 23.

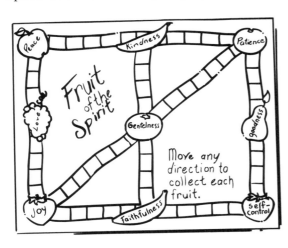

WEEK 2—Harvest Centerpiece

Make a family cornucopia by rounding the edges of a large sheet of brown or yellow poster board to make "almost" a circle. Roll the poster board diagonally to make a cornucopia or "horn of plenty." Glue dried grasses, straw, or raffia onto the horn. Then let family members write the fruit of the Spirit on real fruit, one on each piece of fruit. Place the pieces of fruit in the cornucopia and set the harvest centerpiece on your dining table. At meals, choose a fruit and pass it around the table as you tell how you demonstrated that fruit during the day. Then share the fruit for dessert.

WEEK 4—Bible Search

Have the family cut nine pictures of fruit from old magazines and newspapers. Write a fruit of the Spirit on each fruit. Form family partners and hand each pair two or three paper fruits and a marker or pen. Have partners look up two other references for their words in the Bible. (You'll need a concordance for this!) Write on the paper fruit what the verses say about your words, then read them aloud. When all the pieces of fruit have been read, place them in a small bowl or basket to make a "good fruit bowl" to keep on your dining table. Choose a paper fruit each morning during breakfast and read the words on it. Share a prayer asking for the Holy Spirit's help in demonstrating that fruit during the day in what you say and do.

GIVING THANKS

Colossians 3:16, 17

PLANTING THE SEEDS

As autumn begins to give way to winter, thoughts turn to Thanksgiving and the warm love it creates. In the presence of fragrant pies and family reunions, people suddenly become more aware of the blessings that surround them. In a similar way, Colossians 3:16, 17 remind us of blessings and their source—God. These powerful verses also teach about the attitude of gratitude and thanks we need to nurture as an ongoing lifestyle and not just as a temporary stop on the seasonal calendar.

PRE K–K (Colossians 3:17a). Preschoolers and kindergartners are enthralled with the food, fun, and family Thanksgiving brings. It's a perfect time to teach them that all blessings come from God and that we can give thanks to him each day through Jesus. Help young children begin to develop a thankful lifestyle of being aware of the many things and people we're truly thankful for. Children will be learning the first portion of Colossians 3:17 but will be exposed to the entire verse.

ELEMENTARY (Colossians 3:17). Thanksgiving means lots of eats, treats, family fun, and school vacation! Older kids are thankful for time off from studies and for the fun that surrounds this late autumn holiday. Now stretch their thanks a bit further as they explore what being thankful through Jesus means and why we're to have that same Thanksgiving feeling all year long.

YOUTH/ADULT (Colossians 3:16, 17). Teen and adult learners see and feel the "major" blessings in their lives. From parents and significant others to jobs, cars, or finding money for those extra bills, older learners realize that they have a lot to be thankful for. But what many fail to recognize is the distinct difference between feeling *thankful* and showing *gratitude*. God calls us to do both, and Colossians 3:16, 17 even give us a few ways to accomplish that heartfelt attitude of gratitude!

SECRET SCRIPTURE SIGNAL

Each month a new Scripture signal is suggested as a fun way of signaling someone in your church or family to repeat the month's key verse! This month you'll pat your heart two times. Each time you or someone else pats their heart twice, both of you repeat the verse, then give each other a hearty "thank you!"

GARDENING TIPS

✦ Elementary kids will be using the Scripture window (see the pattern below). This is a great time to use the Scripture window to review verses you've already learned in this book or in class. Simply write the verses on long, 2-inch-wide strips of poster board, then slip them through the window to reveal and cover up parts of the verse as you repeat it.

✦ Consider hosting a Thanksgiving breakfast before church and using the ways of thanking God found in Colossians 3:16, 17. Serve donuts and juice, then sing psalms, hymns, and spiritual songs to praise and thank God for his many blessings in Jesus' name.

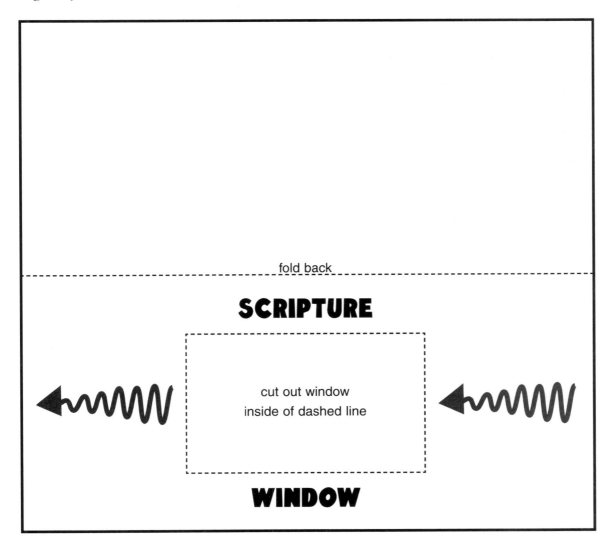

fold back

SCRIPTURE

cut out window
inside of dashed line

WINDOW

WEEK 1—SOWING THE WORD

Photocopy the Fun Family Activities from page 115, one for each child.

Gather children in a circle and tell them you'll be learning a new verse that teaches us about being thankful to God. Point out that Thanksgiving is close and that this time of year especially we want to give God thanks in all we do and say.

Repeat the first and last portions of Colossians 3:17 two times aloud. Then lead children in the following action song to the tune of "Old MacDonald." For the blank, fill in action words such as *clap, hop,* or *turn around.* Sing the song through slowly at first so children become familiar with the words and actions.

> ***In all you do and all you say—*** (Sway back and forth.)
> ***Do it for the Lord!*** (Turn around and clap one time.)
> ***When you work or when you play—*** (Sway back and forth.)
> ***Do it for the Lord!*** (Turn around and clap one time.)
> ***When you*** *(blank)* (Fill in with action word.)
> ***When you sing,***
> ***Give thanks to God for everything!***
> ***In all you do and all you say—***
> ***Do it for the Lord!***

Repeat Colossians 3:17 two times echo-style. Explain that it's important to thank God every day for all he does for us. Share a prayer thanking God for blessings such as family and friends. Then hand out the Fun Family Activities.

WEEK 2—KNOWING THE WORD

For this activity, you'll need colorful crepe paper, tape, markers, aluminum foil, scissors, and a paint stir stick for each child. Cut 12-inch-long strips of aluminum foil and crepe paper, at least six streamers for each child. You'll also need copies of the Scripture Card from page 126 for each child.

Have children sing the Scripture song you learned last week. Let children think up action words to put in the blank. Then repeat Colossians 3:17 three times aloud. Remind children that we're to thank God through Jesus for everything. Tell them that singing to God is a good way to give thanks and that you'll make fun pompons to help with the song and your expression of thanks. Have children tape streamers to the ends of the stir sticks. Let children choose one or both ends! Then help children write "Thanks" along one side of the handle and tape the Scripture Card on the other side.

Play a game in which you mention a person, place, or thing and have children wave their thank-you sticks and shout, "We thank you, God!" Then invite children to name things or people they're thankful for. End by singing the Scripture song once more, waving the sticks in time to the music.

WEEK 3—GROWING THE WORD

You'll need bubbles and blowing wands for this activity. Purchase ready-made bubbles or make them by adding a tablespoon of dish soap and a teaspoon of corn syrup to a half gallon of water. Make blowing wands from chenille wires.

Lead children in repeating Colossians 3:17 two times aloud, then ask:

❧ **Who do we thank through Jesus?** (God)

❧ **What do we thank God for?** (Everything; all things)

❧ **Why do we say thank you to God?** (We love him; he helps us.)

Discuss with children different ways we can give thanks to God, which might include reading and learning his Word, praying, singing, and being kind to others. Then tell children they'll have a chance to say, "Thank you, God" in any words they would like. If it's sunny, go outside for this part of the activity; if not, spread an old shower curtain on the floor and let children say a word of thanks, then blow a bubble. As the bubbles float and fly, point out that our thanks rise to God just as the bubbles rise and that God hears every thank-you and I love you!

End with a prayer expressing your thanks to God for blessings such as church, school, the Bible, and being able to learn about God and Jesus.

WEEK 4—SHOWING THE WORD

You'll need paper, crayons or markers, and glue or tape. Copy the two-line rhyming couplet below for children to glue to the pictures they'll illustrate.

Sing the Scripture song you learned the first week and have children follow along with the actions. Then repeat Colossians 3:17 two times. When you're done, say, "Thank you, God, for helping us remember your Word!"

Remind children that thanking God is important and that you've spent the last few weeks expressing thanks in different ways, such as singing, waving thank-you sticks, and blowing thank-you bubbles. Today kids will draw pictures of something they're especially thankful for, such as families, friends, pets, or flowers. As children draw their pictures, make comments such as "We want to thank God in everything we do and say." Have children glue or tape the two-line prayer on their papers. Read aloud the prayer and have children join in saying, "amen."

 Thank you, God, for all you give— For all the ways you help us live! Amen.

WEEK 1—SOWING THE WORD

Before this activity, photocopy the Scripture window (page 107) on stiff paper for each child. You'll also need to copy the Fun Family Activities on page 115. Cut a 2-by-8-inch strip of poster board. Have markers, tape, and scissors ready. Write Colossians 3:17 on a sheet of newsprint and attach it to the wall or door for kids to read.

Read aloud Colossians 3:17, then have kids repeat the verse aloud two times. Explain that this verse teaches us to give thanks to God in all things and to do and say all things for God. Remind kids that it's almost Thanksgiving time but that we don't thank God just once a year. We thank him through Jesus in all we say and do. Repeat the verse once more.

Distribute the Scripture window pages, then hand kids the poster-board strips and have them write Colossians 3:17 along the length of the strip. Color and cut out the Scripture windows and cut out the windows as indicated on the pattern. Then fold the Scripture windows in half and tape the sides. Cut the end from the Scripture windows so that when the Scripture strips are inserted from right to left, they can be slid through to the left to expose parts of the verse.

Let kids work on learning Colossians 3:17 by exposing portions of the verse and trying to fill in the rest from memory, then sliding the strips through to see if they're correct. Encourage kids to use the Scripture windows at home during the week to learn Colossians 3:17 as a way to thank God for his precious Word! Hand out the Fun Family Activities. Keep the Scripture newsprint to use later on.

WEEK 2—KNOWING THE WORD

For this activity, you'll need paper plates, glue, markers, and old magazines with pictures of food.

Repeat Colossians 3:17 two times aloud, then invite pairs of kids to repeat the verse in sections, taking portions between the commas in the verse. Have partners give each other high fives when they complete the verse. Then ask:

❧ **Why is it important to give thanks in all we do? in all we say?**
❧ **How does thanking God through Jesus demonstrate our love for the Lord?**
❧ **What does it mean to give thanks to God *through* Jesus?**
❧ **What can you give thanks for today?**

Have kids work in small groups to tear out pictures of foods and glue them to paper plates. Write Colossians 3:17 around the rims of the plates, then have kids write one thing they would like to thank God for—such as their families, friends, or God's love—on each food item. Have small groups offer a prayer of thanks by having each person read what he is thankful for, then ending with a corporate "amen." Tell kids to hang their plates in a place they'll see often and be reminded of all they can thank God for in their lives. Close by repeating Colossians 3:17 once more.

WEEK 3—GROWING THE WORD

For this activity you'll need a box, festive wrapping paper, tape, construction paper, markers, and the following foods: a box of mashed potatoes, a box of stuffing, a can of green beans, and a can of cranberry sauce.

Cut the newsprint verse of Colossians 3:17 into as many pieces as there are kids, then see how quickly kids can reassemble the verse. If there's time, have kids choose new puzzles pieces and try to beat their time.

Remind everyone that being thankful is a year-round attitude and that the best way to express gratitude is by helping others. Tell kids they'll prepare a decorated box with wrapped foods to share. Then explain that they'll have a week to collect donations of money to purchase a turkey to place in the box for a needy family. Have some of the kids wrap the food items, have some decorate and wrap the box, and have some make a card using Colossians 3:17.

Finish by sharing a prayer thanking God for his blessings and asking for his help in expressing your thanks through the Thanksgiving feast box. Remind kids to bring their donations next week.

WEEK 4—SHOWING THE WORD

Purchase a frozen turkey before class. Kids will defray the cost through their donations and be able to complete their box and present it to a church leader to give to a needy family.

Begin by repeating Colossians 3:17 two times, then have kids tell ways we can express our thanks to God. Suggestions might include prayer, singing, reading and learning God's Word, and sharing with others. Then have kids gather around the Thanksgiving feast box and pray that God will help you find ways to express your continual thanks through Jesus. End the prayer in Jesus' name.

Collect any donations for the turkey, then let kids add the turkey to the box. Present your expression of thanks to a minister or another church leader to share with a needy family in the church, neighborhood, or community. End by repeating Colossians 3:17.

WEEK 1—SOWING THE WORD

Write Colossians 3:16, 17 on two sheets of newsprint and tape them on the wall. You'll need one copy of the Scripture Card from page 128 and of the Weekly Word Journal from page 114 for each participant. Keep markers or pens nearby.

Invite learners to read Colossians 3:16, 17 one time silently, then have them read the verses two times aloud. Explain that, with Thanksgiving approaching, our thoughts and actions turn toward thanking God for his many blessings. Point out that Colossians 3:16, 17 teaches us to have an "attitude of gratitude" all year long!

Ask learners to identify any patterns or word tricks in these verses, then point out that there is a short list that contains the *phonetic* pattern of s-h-s-s (psalms, hymns, and spiritual songs). Circle the words. Then note that verse 16 begins with Jesus and verse 17 ends with Jesus. Underline the word *Christ* in verse 16 and *him* in verse 17. Finally, point out that the last phrase in verse 16 has *gratitude,* while the last phrase in verse 17 has *thanks.* Have learners circle and underline all these patterns on their Scripture Cards.

Challenge learners to tape their Scripture Cards to their bathroom mirrors or the dashboards of their cars to practice during stoplights and traffic slow-downs. Hand out the Weekly Word Journals.

WEEK 2—KNOWING THE WORD

Photocopy the question box from this activity, one for every three people. Be sure to have pens available.

Repeat Colossians 3:16, 17 two times aloud. Remind everyone that these verses teach us about thanks and gratitude for all situations and in all our actions and words. Invite learners to form trios and hand each trio a pen and question box. Encourage groups to discuss the questions, then be prepared to share with the entire group.

If time permits, ask people to share their insights. Close by sharing a prayer thanking God for blessings in your lives. Invite each learner to name one blessing for which she is thankful. Then close in Jesus' name.

Thanks and Gratitude

❧ What is the difference between *thanks* and *gratitude?*
❧ Which is indicative of action and which is a feeling? Explain.
❧ How are thanks and gratitude related? Why do we need both?
❧ How are thanks and gratitude expressions of love for God?
❧ Why do we go through Jesus to express our thanks to God?
❧ How can the "word of Christ" help us thank God?

Let the word of Christ dwell in you.... And whatever you do ... do it all in the name of the Lord.... Colossians 3:16, 17

WEEK 3—GROWING THE WORD

You'll need envelopes, stamps, and pens for this activity. Cut sheets of paper in half so each person will have two halves. You may also want to have on hand a local phone book in which you can look up addresses.

Cut the two verses on newsprint into as many puzzle pieces as there are participants. Hand out the puzzle pieces and challenge learners to reassemble Colossians 3:16, 17 in as little time as possible. Repeat the verse two times aloud, then ask:

> ❧ **How does demonstrating our gratitude, as opposed to just feeling thankful, show our love to God?**
> ❧ **What are some specific ways we can God show our gratitude?**
> ❧ **How is serving or sharing with someone a way to show gratitude?**

Explain that verse 17 says we're to thank God through Jesus. Remind everyone that loving others is the best way to serve Jesus and that we can thank God for his grace by showing kindness to others. Hand each person two pieces of paper, an envelope, a stamp, and a pen. Challenge learners to write two thank-you notes: one to a special someone and one to God. Encourage people to be specific with their thanks and to be sure their feelings come from the heart, as Colossians 3:16 tells us.

Put the thank-you notes to people into envelopes and have learners address them and add a stamp. Challenge learners to read their thank-you notes to God aloud to families or friends or at bedtime as a thank-you prayer. Be sure to mail the thank-you notes as you watch what a few sincere words of thanks can do to spread God's love!

WEEK 4—SHOWING THE WORD

Invite pairs of learners to repeat Colossians 3:16, 17 together, with each person repeating one verse. Then have each pair join another pair and repeat the verse. Continue until everyone is in one group repeating Colossians 3:16, 17 together.

Have learners return to their original partners and hand each pair a sheet of paper and a pen. Invite partners to quietly read Psalm 100, then explain that this psalm was written as a thank-you to God for his blessings and power. Point out how praise is closely related to thanks. Then challenge partners to compose a psalm of thanksgiving to honor and thank God. Have learners end their psalms with, "Thanks be to God through our Lord Jesus!"

When pairs are finished writing their psalms, let partners share their work with the whole group. After each psalm is read, lead everyone in repeating a corporate "amen" so that the psalms become prayers of thanksgiving.

If possible, quickly photocopy each psalm for every person, then collect them into a small booklet and staple the corner. Challenge everyone to read a psalm a day for the next few weeks as a joyous expression of thanks and a reminder that every day is Thanksgiving when we honor God! End by repeating Colossians 3:16, 17. (If necessary, create and distribute the "psalm books" at a later time.)

November

WEEK 1

Read Colossians 3:16, 17 and think for a moment about the words *thanks* and *gratitude* used in these verses. John Newton wrote the words to "Amazing Grace" because he was passionate about the thanks and profound gratitude he felt for God. Because God wrought an amazing act of grace, John Newton wrote notes of amazing gratitude! Kick off the Thanksgiving season and your study of Colossians 3:16, 17 by honoring God with one act of amazing gratitude for someone this week. Perhaps you might purchase lunch for a group of teens you don't know or paint the fence of an elderly neighbor. On the back of this page, write your amazing gratitude game plan, then commit to carrying it out this week.

WEEK 2

Read Colossians 3:16, 17 and underline the three action words in verse 16. We often think of *thanks* as more passive than *gratitude*. In fact, thanks is the feeling that leads us to acts of gratitude. Now answer these questions.

❧ Why must someone feel thankful before he or she reaches the level called "gratitude"?

_____
_____

❧ Is it adequate to have just a feeling of thankfulness? Why or why not?

_____
_____

❧ What can you *do* tomorrow to show gratitude to God for all he has done in your life?

_____
_____

WEEK 3

Colossians 3:17 teaches us to thank God through Jesus. What else is given to God or received from God through Jesus? Read the verses on the left and draw matching lines to the correct answers on the right.

Romans 5:17	salvation
Hebrews 13:15	victory
Galatians 3:26	wisdom
1 Corinthians 15:57	grace & righteousness
Romans 16:27	faith
2 Timothy 3:15	glory
1 Thessalonians 5:9	praise

WEEK 4

Colossians 3:16, 17 teaches us to give thanks and show gratitude to God. Read Job 1:20-22; 2:10; and 1 Thessalonians 5:18. Then answer the following questions on the back.

❧ How is it possible to be truly thankful even in hard times—or is it?

❧ How does giving thanks *through Jesus* help us be grateful to God even in the most difficult situations?

❧ How can we be sure our gratitude comes from our hearts, as Colossians 3:16 teaches?

❧ What role does faith play in thanks and gratitude? What role does love play?

❧ Write several sentences explaining what Job meant in Job 2:10. Then explain how we can have an attitude of gratitude even when we're in times of trouble.

November

WEEK 1—Thank Bank

Make a family bank to express your thanks to God. Purchase an inexpensive but festive-looking piggy bank (the kind with a stopper on the bottom to remove coins). Then cut out paper coins and have each person write one way to thank God on one side of the coin and something they're thankful for on the other side. (Young children can dictate their responses to adults.) Have each person make two or three paper coins. Deposit the coins in the bank and place the bank  on your dinner table. At each meal, remove a coin and have the family express their thanks to God for the blessing on the coin in the way the coin states. Continue until all the coins have been "spent."

WEEK 3—Pumpkin Bars

What a perfect time of year to thank God for good foods. Have the whole family help make—and eat—these spicy-good bars! You'll need a small package of white cake mix, 3 tablespoons cinnamon, canned pumpkin, powdered sugar, and raisins.

Prepare the cake mix according to package directions but substitute one cup of canned pumpkin for the liquid in the directions. Stir in the cinnamon and a half cup of raisins (add chopped walnuts if you desire). Spread the batter in an oblong pan and bake according to the package directions. When the bars are hot from the oven, sprinkle them with powdered sugar. Mmm good!

WEEK 2—Praise Prayer

Read aloud Psalm 100. Then compose your own family praise prayer to repeat at meals and during devotion times. Use the pattern below or create your own by having each family member supply a thank-you in the prayer. Write the prayer on poster board and decorate it. Then hang the poster in a place your family gathers often until everyone has learned it by heart!

Our family thanks you, Father above,
For your perfect power and awesome love!
Thank you for . . . (add thank-yous here).
Our gratitude and love burn like the brightest flame—
And we give you thanks, O Lord, in Jesus' precious name! Amen.

WEEK 4—Three-Second Thanks!

Have each family member say, "Thank you, God, in Jesus' name. I love you!" as you time that person with a watch with a second hand. It should take about three seconds to repeat those simple yet powerful words! Remind family members that it only takes a few seconds to thank God through Jesus and that Colossians 3:17 tells us to thank God in all we say and do. Take turns writing other three-second thank-yous to God through Jesus, such as, "In Jesus' name I give you thanks, O Lord." Time the suggestions to see if they're about three seconds long. Have everyone choose a three-second thank-you to repeat often during the week. Change your thank-yous next week.

CHRISTMAS

PLANTING THE SEEDS

Holiday smiles, glittering tinsel, and laughter and love as prevalent as presents under the tree mark the Christmas season. It's time to celebrate the birthday of the world's most glorious gift of love—Jesus! But in the hubbub of shopping, cooking, and cleaning for holiday guests, there's not much time to contemplate *why* God sent Jesus into the world, *what* his gift of grace truly did for us, or the result of his selfless love. John 3:16 is perhaps the best-known, most loved verse in the Bible, but verses 17 and 18 continue the story of God's perfect plan for our redemption. What timeless verses to contemplate as you delight in the joys of the season!

PRE K–K (John 3:16a). Young children are all aglow over the wonders of Christmas and the anticipation of gifts and fun. It's hard to get them to calm down long enough to sleep let alone learn Bible verses! But if children understand that Jesus is a gift sent by God to love and forgive us, they begin to see how, without Jesus and his love, there is no reason to celebrate at all! Children will be learning the first portion of John 3:16 but will be exposed to the entire verse through an easy-to-learn song.

ELEMENTARY (John 3:16). Older kids love Christmas as much as preschoolers and can hardly contain their excitement at the prospect of discovering the secret contents of beautiful packages. It's so hard to wait! Help kids realize that the gift of love and forgiveness Jesus brought into the world are gifts that we don't need to wait for! John 3:16 may be familiar to some kids, but it is a verse that's worth reviewing, celebrating, and applying.

YOUTH/ADULT (John 3:16-18). It seems the older we get, the more apt we are to feel or say, "Bah, humbug!" at the thought of hectic Christmas parties, costly shopping, and hours of wrapping gifts. This year, help older learners celebrate the joy that comes with the gift of freedom from condemnation and really contemplate the gift that Jesus' justification and love bring. Older learners will be exploring the concept of "belief" and how it applies to condemnation and salvation through the best Christmas gift we'll ever have—without hours of wrapping and with a bill that has already been paid!

SECRET SCRIPTURE SIGNAL

Each month a new Scripture signal is suggested as a fun way of signaling someone in your church or family to repeat the month's key verse! For this month's Scripture signal, you'll say the words, "Show me the gift!" Each time you or a friend says, "Show me the gift!" repeat John 3:16, then end by giving each other the gift of a warm hug or a loving pat on the shoulders!

GARDENING TIPS

✦ Wrap each word to John 3:16 (or 17 and 18) in festive paper and pass the words around a circle. Unwrap the "gifts" and reassemble the verse. Chat about why God's Word is also a gift to us.

✦ Write the words to John 3:16 on small Christmas ornament balls, then hang them on a class tree. Read the verse by pointing to the ornaments each time you are together!

✦ Bring in jingle bells and put the words to John 3:16 to familiar Christmas songs such as "The First Noel" and "Jingle Bells." Ring the bells as you sing the words to the verse. (It may be a bit contrived, but when you're in a joyful holiday spirit, who minds?)

WEEK I—SOWING THE WORD

Before this activity, photocopy and enlarge the rebus pictures on page 117, using only the pictures in the illustration below. Color the pictures and assemble the verse on a sheet of poster board. Be sure the poster is placed where children can see and point to the pictures. You'll also need to photocopy the Fun Family Activities from page 125 and the Scripture Card from page 126 for each child.

Gather children by the rebus poster for John 3:16a. Point to the pictures as you say, "For God so loved the world that he gave his one and only Son." Repeat the verse two times as you point to the pictures. Then repeat the verse but let children say the picture words. Explain that this verse is one of the best-loved verses in the Bible because it tells us why God sent Jesus to love us. Remind children that Christmas is the time we celebrate Jesus' birthday and the love and forgiveness he brought us.

Teach children the following action song sung to the tune of "The Farmer in the Dell." Sing the song three times until children become familiar with the words. If there's time, sing the song slowly as you point to the corresponding pictures on the poster.

> ***For God so loved the world*** (Hug yourself.)
> ***He gave his only Son,*** (Put hands out in front of you.)
> ***That whosoever shall believe*** (Pat your heart.)
> ***Shall have eternal life.*** (Point upwards.)

Hand out the Fun Family Activities and Scripture Cards and remind children to practice their verse this week with their families.

WEEK 2—KNOWING THE WORD

Prior to this activity, collect red and yellow paint pens or permanent markers and a large white satin Christmas ball ornament for each child.

Sing the Scripture song from last week, then repeat the first portion of John 3:16 as kids take turns pointing to the pictures on the rebus poster. Remind children that God loved us so much that he sent his Son Jesus to give us the gift of forever life. Point to the heart on the poster and ask children to tell what a heart signifies. Then point to the cross and ask what a cross stands for. Tell children that they'll make Christmas balls to remind them of God's love and how he sent Jesus to love us, too.

Hand each child a white satin ornament. Help children outline red hearts with yellow crosses inside on their ornaments. As the ornaments dry, tell children that God wanted us to live with him forever, so Jesus came to forgive our sins and let us live with God in heaven. Repeat John 3:16a again, then close with a prayer thanking God for his wonderful gift of live in Jesus. Have kids take home their Christmas ornaments.

WEEK 3—GROWING THE WORD

Before this activity, wrap a small gift for each child. Gift ideas might include small plastic crosses to set on their dressers, small Bibles, small Bible story books, or balls with crosses or hearts on them. Be sure the small packages look festive and bright!

Repeat John 3:16 as children take turns pointing to the pictures on the rebus poster, then sing the Scripture song based on John 3:16 two times. Ask children:

➤ **Who sent Jesus to us?** (God)

➤ **Why did God send Jesus?** (He loved us; to let us live forever with God)

Set the gifts on the floor. Tell children that God sent us the very first Christmas gift when he sent Jesus to love us. Explain that God wanted us to have the gift of Jesus right away and not wait like we do for most Christmas presents. Help each child repeat the first portion of John 3:16, then say, "God loves you so much!" as you hand each child a gift to open.

As children admire their small gifts, tell them to think of God's love and the gift of Jesus each time they see their special gifts. Close by singing the Scripture song one time. Keep the boxes the gifts were wrapped in to use next week.

WEEK 4—SHOWING THE WORD

You'll need drawing paper and markers, festive gift wrap, stick-on bows, scissors, tape, and the gift boxes from last week. You'll also need a copy of the Scripture Card from page 126 for each child.

Lead children in singing the Scripture song you learned earlier, then challenge children to repeat John 3:16a. If needed, give a word or two to start them. Then ask:

➤ **How does it feel to know God loves you so much?**

➤ **What do we say to someone who gives us a special gift?** (thank you)

➤ **How can we thank God for his special gift of Jesus?**

Suggestions might include singing God a song, drawing him a picture, learning God's Word, and being kind to others.

Remind children that Christmas is the celebration of Jesus' birth—like his birthday! Tell children they can make birthday presents for Jesus by drawing pictures of how happy and glad they are to have Jesus in their lives. When the pictures are complete, help children tape the Scripture Cards to them. Then let children put their pictures in the boxes and wrap them with gift wrap and bows. Challenge children to unwrap the presents for Jesus on Christmas and hang the pictures in their rooms to remind them of their joy in the perfect gift of Jesus!

WEEK 1—SOWING THE WORD

Prior to this activity, enlarge and photocopy the rebus pictures for John 3:16 on page 117. Make one set of regular-sized pictures for each child and a set to use on a large poster. Color and cut out the enlarged pictures and glue them to a sheet of poster board. Add the words to the verse as shown in the illustration. Attach the poster to a wall or door. You'll need markers, scissors, tape, and smaller pieces of poster board so kids can make their own rebus posters. Photocopy the Fun Family Activities from page 125 for each child.

Gather kids by the rebus Scripture poster of John 3:16 and explain that some of them might already know this verse, since it's one of the most loved verses in all God's Word. Give kids a moment to see if they can decipher the rebus pictures, then repeat John 3:16 as you point at the pictures. Explain that this verse is perfect for Christmastime because it tells us what God's greatest gift to us was: Jesus. Tell kids that, to celebrate the reason for the season, they'll make their own rebus Scripture posters to hang by their Christmas trees at home.

Let kids work in pairs to color and cut out the rebus pictures, tape them to poster board, and add the words to the verse. End by having kids point to the posters as they repeat the verse to their partners. Hand out the Fun Family Activities.

WEEK 2—KNOWING THE WORD

Gather gold glitter squeeze paint, green fabric paint, and one large blue Christmas ornament ball for each child plus one extra. Paint the extra ornament as a sample. You'll be painting "land' on the blue "waters" of the ornament to make the world. When the green paint is dry or at least tacky (after several minutes) use gold glitter squeeze paint to make a cross on each half of the ornament.

Have kids repeat John 3:16 using the rebus poster, then invite volunteers to repeat the verse with no more than two peeks. Ask:

✦ **How was Jesus a demonstration of God's love?**

✦ **In what ways is Jesus our greatest gift of life and love?**

✦ **Why is it vital to believe in Jesus and his saving love?**

Remind kids that Jesus is the reason for the season of Christmas. Hold up the ornament you made earlier and tell kids they'll make neat ornaments to remind them that Jesus came into the world to love us and save us from sin. Have kids form pairs and make ornaments. After the ornaments are finished, share a prayer thanking God for his gift of Jesus in your lives, then repeat John 3:16 once more.

For God so loved the world that he gave his one and only Son, that whoever believes in him shall not perish.... John 3:16

WEEK 3—GROWING THE WORD

Before this activity, wrap a small gift for each child. Gifts might include small Bibles, crosses to place on their dressers or desks, pencil and eraser sets, or small toys. Make one copy of the rebus pictures from page 117 for every two kids. Color and cut out the pictures and place each set in an envelope.

Have kids form pairs or trios. Hand each group an envelope. Challenge kids to reassemble the pictures in order, then pop up, repeat the verse, and give each other high fives. Have kids tell the significance of each rebus picture, such as the cloud representing God, who sent his only Son to us.

Line the packages up on the floor and gather kids around them. Tell kids that we have to wait for most Christmas gifts to be opened but that Jesus is our TBOE gift: To Be Opened Early! Ask:

❧ **Why do we want to accept the gift of Jesus right away and not wait?**

❧ **What has Jesus done for us by coming to love and forgive us?**

❧ **In what ways is Jesus' salvation a gift to us? to the world?**

As you pass the gifts around the circle, have kids tell ways Jesus is a gift to us from God. Then let kids open the gifts as a reminder that Jesus Christ is our TBOE gift and that we want to unwrap his love today! Set aside the boxes the gifts were wrapped in to use next week.

WEEK 4—SHOWING THE WORD

For this activity you'll gift wrap, stick-on bows, tape, scissors, markers, and paper. You'll also need a copy of the Scripture Card from page 127 for each child and the gift boxes from last week.

Have groups of four kids repeat John 3:16, with each taking a different phrase: "For God so loved the world," "that he gave his one and only Son," "that whoever believes in him shall not perish," "but have eternal life." Continue until everyone has had a turn to repeat one portion, then repeat the entire verse once in unison. Remind kids that Jesus is the greatest gift we'll ever receive and that Christmas is really Jesus' birthday celebration! Ask:

❧ **What gifts can we give to Jesus to celebrate his birth this year?**

Suggestions might include reading the Bible, being helpful and kind, or learning God's Word. Have kids write or draw on paper what they'd like to give Jesus as a gift, or have kids write Jesus a love note or praise poem. Then place the papers inside the boxes and wrap them. Challenge kids to unwrap their gifts to Jesus on Christmas Day and to be sure to honor their gifts by doing what their papers say.

Close by sharing a prayer thanking Jesus for being our perfect gift of love and salvation. End by repeating John 3:16 two times.

WEEK 1—SOWING THE WORD

Before this activity, write John 3:16-18 on three sheets of newsprint, one verse per page. Display the verses in a place where everyone can read them. Photocopy the Scripture Card from page 128 and the Weekly Word Journal from page 124 for each person. You'll also need markers or pens.

Have everyone silently read John 3:16-18, then explain that, because verse 16 is the most well-loved portion of Scripture, they probably know it already, at least in part. Point out that these three verses give the entire reason for the Christmas season. Hand out the Scripture Cards and pens. Have someone read aloud verse 16 and decide whether this is a verse that tells us what God did, why he did it, or what the result of his action is. (Verse 16 tells what God did for us.) Write the word *WHAT* beside the verse and have learners do the same on their Scripture Cards.

Then read aloud verse 17 and decide if it tells the *why* or the *result* of God's action. (Verse 17 tells why God sent Jesus.) Write *WHY* in the margin beside verse 17. Finally, write the word *RESULT* beside verse 18.

Challenge learners to use these memory keys to learn these three longer and challenging verses before next week. Distribute the Weekly Word Journals.

WEEK 2—KNOWING THE WORD

Prepare a wooden cross on a stand for each person. Use the illustration as an example. If you can't cut wooden crosses, use thick branches and tie them with twine to make crosses. Nail each cross to a large wooden rectangle. You'll also need six small cup hooks for each person and copies of the Scripture Card from page 128.

Have everyone repeat John 3:16-18 two times together (using the newsprint as needed), then invite trios to each repeat one of the verses. Remind learners about the why, the what, and the result. Then point out that verse 17 contains the word *world* three times and that verse 18 has a form of *believe* in it three times. Then have learners form small groups to answer these questions:

➤ **How was Jesus a demonstration of God's love for the world?**
➤ **What would be different if God had sent Jesus to condemn the world?**
➤ **Considering John 3:16-18, how are Christmas and Easter related?**

Explain that other classes are making ornaments to remind them that Jesus came into the world with love and forgiveness. To portray that Christmas and Easter are related, learners will make Christmas crosses to hang the ornaments on. Have learners attach six cup hooks to their crosses (three on each side). Glue the Scripture Card for John 3:16-18 on the wooden base. Tell learners to hang ornaments on the Christmas crosses to remind them that Jesus' birth, life, death, and resurrection are the real reasons for the season. End by repeating John 3:16-18 one time.

For God so loved the world that he gave his one and only Son, that whoever believes in him shall not perish.... John 3:16-18

WEEK 3—GROWING THE WORD

Prior to this activity, wrap small bookmarks for learners. To make bookmarks, purchase tiny cross charms and tie 8-inch lengths of purple satin ribbon or silk cord to the charms. You'll also need copies of the Greatest Gifts box.

Form pairs and have each partner repeat John 3:16-18. Then have each pair join another pair and repeat the verses together. Continue joining small groups until the entire group repeats John 3:16-18 in unison. Have learners return to their original partners and hand each pair a copy of the Greatest Gifts handout and a pen. Instruct learners to look up the references to discover in what ways Jesus was God's greatest gift to us. Then open the gifts to remind everyone of the gifts that Jesus has brought us through his life and death. Keep the gift boxes to use next week.

GREATEST GIFTS

Isn't it amazing that at Jesus' first birthday celebration a multitude of gifts were given *to us?* Look up the references below, then list the gifts Jesus gave us.

➤ John 10:10, 28 _____

➤ Romans 5:15, 17 _____

➤ 2 Timothy 3:15 _____

➤ 1 Corinthians 15:57 _____

WEEK 4—SHOWING THE WORD

You'll need wrapping paper, tape, stick-on bows, scissors, paper, markers, and the gift boxes from last week.

Repeat John 3:16-18 one time together. Summarize the verses as follows: God sent his only Son Jesus [what] to save the world [why], so any who believe in Jesus will have eternal life [result]. Ask participants how we should respond to such glorious gifts. Hand each person an empty box, a sheet of paper, and a marker. Challenge learners to list two gifts they can give to Jesus in the coming days. Have one gift be something they can do for someone else and one gift that is between them and Jesus, such as doing a personal Bible study. Instruct learners to place their completed "gift lists" in the gift boxes. Wrap the boxes with gift wrap and pretty bows.

Form a circle and have learners hold their gifts to Jesus. Challenge everyone to open the gift for Jesus on Christmas Day and to carry out the gift plans. Close with the following prayer: **Dear Lord, we thank you for the most perfect and precious gift we'll ever receive—the gift of your Son, Jesus Christ. Please help us live in a thankful way and carry out our gift plans to ...** (silently name the two gifts). **In Jesus' name, amen.**

December

WEEK I

Read John 3:16-18. Now use the verse references to fill in the blanks below to discover the WHAT WHY, and RESULT of Jesus' birth.

WHAT God did in sending Jesus (John 3:16)

_____

WHAT we did to need Jesus (Romans 3:23)

_____

WHY God sent Jesus (John 3:17)

_____

WHY we should believe in Jesus (Acts 4:12)

_____

RESULT of God sending Jesus (John 3:18)

_____

RESULT of following Jesus (Ephesians 2:8-10)

_____

WEEK 2

Read John 3:16, 17. These verses teach that God sent Jesus to save the world and to give us eternal life. Look up the following verses and write other reasons Jesus gave for why he came into the world.

➤ Luke 19:10

_____
_____

➤ Mark 10:45

_____
_____

➤ John 6:38

_____
_____

➤ John 10:10

_____

WEEK 3

Read John 3:18. What is the relation between belief and condemnation? Refer to the references in parentheses to answer these questions on the back of this page:

➤ Can we be condemned if we know, love, and follow Jesus? (Romans 8:1)

➤ What happens when we believe in Jesus and call upon his name? (Acts 16:31)

➤ We were condemned by one act of sin; what one act justified us to God and brought us life? (Romans 5:18)

➤ Write a brief paragraph describing your belief in Jesus as the one and only Son of God and how this brings you eternal life, then write a few sentences outlining how you can help someone else believe in the name of Jesus and in his power to forgive sins.

WEEK 4

Christmastime seems to revolve around gifts and presents and the excitement of discovering what's inside each pretty package. The irony is that on someone's birthday we bring gifts to celebrate their special day, yet on Jesus' birthday we spend so much time gifting others! This year, commit to giving Jesus a gift of love by learning one of the most powerful and life-giving statements Jesus made! Write, repeat, learn, and use John 11:25, 26 and set a goal of learning these verses during the week of and immediately following Christmas. Then help a loved one learn the verses, too. What a perfect gift of love for our gift of love—Jesus!

Jesus said to her, "I am the resurrection and the life. He who believes in me will live, even though he dies; and whoever lives and believes in me will never die. Do you believe this?"
(John 11:25, 26).

December

WEEK 1—Tell 'Em Today!

Let family members help others know the great news about Jesus' birth and the reason God sent us this special gift! Draw the simple icons below on paper plates so they're BIG, then color them brightly. Glue the paper plates to a bright, solid-colored plastic shower curtain. Write out the words to the verse in black permanent marker, then hang your cool banner on the side of your house, porch, or garage for everyone to see, read, and enjoy!

WEEK 3—Christ Cookies

Make unusual Christmas cookies to remind everyone that Jesus came to love and save the world. Purchase ready-made sugar cookies and spread them with blue and green icing to make cookies that look like the world. When the icing is a bit dried, use red squirt-tube icing to draw hearts and yellow tube icing to make crosses on the cookies. Finish by sprinkling a touch of granulated sugar on the cookies to add sparkle. Prepare plates of these lovely cookies to give as gifts to friends and neighbors. Be sure to add cards with John 3:16 on them!

WEEK 2—Silent Night

Celebrate Jesus' first birthday by making cute Christmas ornaments to hang on your Christmas crosses, Christmas tree, or as gift toppers. For each ornament, glue three craft sticks into a triangle. Place the triangle so it's pointing upward. Next, tear colored construction paper into the following shapes: a manger, baby Jesus, Mary, Joseph. Glue the figures to the bottom of the triangle "stable" and place a shiny star sticker at the top of the triangle. Tie a loop of fishing line through the top of the triangle so the ornament can be hung. You may wish to write John 3:16 along the three sides of the craft-stick stable.

WEEK 4—Verse Review

Play a fun game similar to Old Maid using the icons from John 3:16 in week one of this page. Draw icons on index-card halves and prepare one set for each family member. Shuffle the cards and place them face down. Take turns choosing cards until all the cards are in players' hands. Then take turns picking cards from other players. The object is not to make pairs but to make the entire verse. When you have the verse, place the cards down and repeat John 3:16. Play a variation by placing all the cards face down in rows and taking turns turning over two cards at a time. Keep any pairs of icons you match.

PRE K–K SCRIPTURE CARDS

"Therefore, if anyone is in Christ, he is a new creation; the old has gone, the new has come!" (2 Corinthians 5:17).

"There is but one God, the Father ... and there is but one Lord, Jesus Christ" (1 Corinthians 8:6).

"Neither height nor depth, nor anything else in all creation, will be able to separate us from the love of God that is in Christ Jesus our Lord" (Romans 8:39).

"God will be with you wherever you go" (Joshua 1:9b).

"God has poured out his love into our hearts by the Holy Spirit"(Romans 5:5b).

"All Scripture is God-breathed and is useful" (2 Timothy 3:16a).

"While we were still sinners, Christ died for us" (Romans 5:8b).

"But the fruit of the Spirit is love, joy, peace" (Galatians 5:22a).

"Rejoice in the Lord always. I will say it again: Rejoice!" (Philippians 4:4).

"And whatever you do ... give thanks to God the Father" (Colossians 3:17).

"Encourage one another and build each other up" (1 Thessalonians 5:11a).

"For God so loved the world that he gave his one and only Son" (John 3:16a).

ELEMENTARY SCRIPTURE CARDS

"Therefore, if anyone is in Christ, he is a new creation; the old has gone, the new has come!" (2 Corinthians 5:17).

"Yet for us there is but one God, the Father, from whom all things came and for whom we live; and there is but one Lord, Jesus Christ, through whom all things came and through whom we live"(1 Corinthians 8:6).

"For I am convinced that neither death nor life ... nor anything else in all creation, will be able to separate us from the love of God that is in Christ Jesus our Lord" (Romans 8:38, 39).

"Have I not commanded you? Be strong and courageous. Do not be terrified; do not be discouraged, for the LORD your God will be with you wherever you go" (Joshua 1:9).

"Not only so, but we also rejoice in our sufferings, because we know that suffering produces perseverance; perseverance, character; and character, hope. And hope does not disappoint us, because God has poured out his love into our hearts by the Holy Spirit, whom he has given us" (Romans 5:3-5).

"All Scripture is God-breathed and is useful for teaching, rebuking, correcting and training in righteousness" (2 Timothy 3:16).

"But God demonstrates his own love for us in this: While we were still sinners, Christ died for us" (Romans 5:8).

"But the fruit of the Spirit is love, joy, peace, patience, kindness, goodness, faithfulness, gentleness and self-control. Against such things there is no law" (Galatians 5:22, 23).

"Rejoice in the Lord always. I will say it again: Rejoice! Let your gentleness be evident to all. The Lord is near" (Philippians 4:4, 5).

"And whatever you do, whether in word or deed, do it all in the name of the Lord Jesus, giving thanks to God the Father through him" (Colossians 3:17).

"He died for us so that, whether we are awake or asleep, we may live together with him. Therefore encourage one another and build each other up, just as in fact you are doing" (1 Thessalonians 5:10, 11).

"For God so loved the world that he gave his one and only Son, that whoever believes in him shall not perish but have eternal life" (John 3:16).

YOUTH/ADULT SCRIPTURE CARDS

"Therefore, if anyone is in Christ, he is a new creation; the old has gone, the new has come! All this is from God, who reconciled us to himself through Christ and gave us the ministry of reconciliation; that God was reconciling the world to himself in Christ, not counting men's sins against them. And he has committed to us the message of reconciliation" (2 Corinthians 5:17-19).

"For even if there are so-called gods, whether in heaven or on earth (as indeed there are many 'gods' and many 'lords'), yet for us there is but one God, the Father, from whom all things came and for whom we live; and there is but one Lord, Jesus Christ, through whom all things came and through whom we live" (1 Corinthians 8:5, 6).

"No, in all these things we are more than conquerors through him who loved us. For I am convinced that neither death nor life, neither angels nor demons, neither the present nor the future, nor any powers, neither height nor depth, nor anything else in all creation, will be able to separate us from the love of God that is in Christ Jesus our Lord" (Romans 8:37-39).

"Do not let this Book of the Law depart from your mouth; meditate on it day and night, so that you may be careful to do everything written in it. Then you will be prosperous and successful. Have I not commanded you? Be strong and courageous. Do not be terrified; do not be discouraged, for the LORD your God will be with you wherever you go" (Joshua 1:8, 9).

"Not only so, but we also rejoice in our sufferings, because we know that suffering produces perseverance; perseverance, character; and character, hope. And hope does not disappoint us, because God has poured out his love into our hearts by the Holy Spirit, whom he has given us" (Romans 5:3-5).

"All Scripture is God-breathed and is useful for teaching, rebuking, correcting and training in righteousness, so that the man of God may be thoroughly equipped for every good work" (2 Timothy 3:16, 17).

"Very rarely will anyone die for a righteous man, though for a good man someone might possibly dare to die. But God demonstrates his own love for us in this: While we were still sinners, Christ died for us" (Romans 5:7, 8).

"But the fruit of the Spirit is love, joy, peace, patience, kindness, goodness, faithfulness, gentleness and self-control. Against such things there is no law.... Since we live by the Spirit, let us keep in step with the Spirit" (Galatians 5:22, 23, 25).

"Rejoice in the Lord always. I will say it again: Rejoice! Let your gentleness be evident to all. The Lord is near. Do not be anxious about anything, but in everything, by prayer and petition, with thanksgiving, present your requests to God. And the peace of God, which transcends all understanding, will guard your hearts and your minds in Christ Jesus" (Philippians 4:4-7).

"Let the word of Christ dwell in you richly as you teach and admonish one another with all wisdom, and as you sing psalms, hymns and spiritual songs with gratitude in your hearts to God. And whatever you do, whether in word or deed, do it all in the name of the Lord Jesus, giving thanks to God the Father through him" (Colossians 3:16, 17).

"For God did not appoint us to suffer wrath but to receive salvation through our Lord Jesus Christ. He died for us so that, whether we are awake or asleep, we may live together with him. Therefore encourage one another and build each other up, just as in fact you are doing" (1 Thessalonians 5:9-11).

"For God so loved the world that he gave his one and only Son, that whoever believes in him shall not perish but have eternal life. For God did not send his Son into the world to condemn the world, but to save the world through him. Whoever believes in him is not condemned, but whoever does not believe stands condemned already because he has not believed in the name of God's one and only Son" (John 3:16-18).